Day-End Stories

By

Wes Fulton

Copyright

© 2015-2019, James W. (Wes) Fulton.

All Rights Reserved.

First Edition 2015

Second Edition 2019

Dedication

To my beautiful wife, Mary.

Special thanks to my son, Tom, for giving me the idea.

ROC n ROL Day-End Stories

1. ROC n ROL With Aiden
2. ROC n ROL With Blake
3. ROC n ROL With Cora
4. ROC n ROL With Davella
5. ROC n ROL With Emma
6. ROC n ROL With Fred
7. ROC n ROL With Grace
8. ROC n ROL With Haku
9. ROC n ROL With Isidro
10. ROC n ROL With John
11. ROC n ROL With Kaito
12. ROC n ROL With Lakeesha
13. ROC n ROL With Manu
14. ROC n ROL With Ning
15. ROC n ROL With Olga
16. ROC n ROL With Pradeep
17. ROC n ROL With Quon
18. ROC n ROL With Ringo
19. ROC n ROL With Sachi
20. ROC n ROL With Tai
21. ROC n ROL With Ulan
22. ROC n ROL With Vandita
23. ROC n ROL With Willray
24. ROC n ROL With Xylia
25. ROC n ROL With Yasin
26. ROC n ROL With Zetta

1. ROC n ROL

With Aiden

By

Wes Fulton

Number 1 of 26 in Series

ROC n ROL

Day-End Stories

By

Wes Fulton

Aiden walked to school every morning for Mr. Ha-dro-va-nich's class.

All of the students in Mr. Ha-dro-va-nich's class called him "Mr. H", a shorter and easier name to say. They all liked him because he made their school time fun.

When Aiden arrived at school, he saw Mr. H in front of the school talking with a well-dressed lady. Aiden wondered why they were talking.

The school bell rang, "BBBRRRINNGGG." Aiden was the first to get inside Mr. H's classroom and sit down.

The rest of the class came in and sat down.

Mr. H and the well-dressed lady came into the classroom and went to the front.

Mr. H introduced his good friend, Miss Quick, to the class. "Everyone, this is my good friend, Miss Quick." he said. Miss Quick waved to everybody in the class.

Then Ms. Quick clapped her hands together. CLAP!!!!!

Suddenly there was sparkling dust all around Miss Quick. Nobody could see her behind the sparkles.

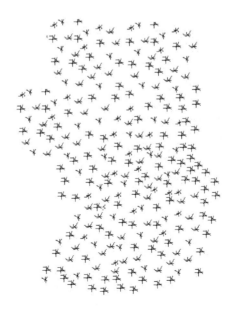

One second later, the dust settled to the floor, Ms. Quick appeared, and she was wearing a completely different dress. The class was amazed.

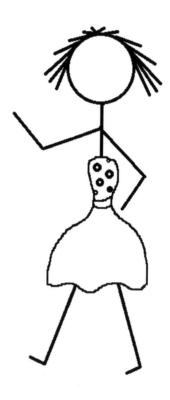

Mr. H explained what just happened.

Mr. H said to the class "Miss Quick performs in a magic act. She is a quick-change artist. She changes her clothes in less than one second."

She clapped her hands again. CLAP!!!!!

There was sparkling dust all around Miss Quick again.

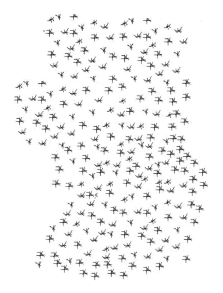

She appeared one second later wearing something else completely different.

The whole class laughed and clapped their hands.

"Some change is fast, and other change is slow." said Miss Quick.

Miss Quick told the class "Today, Mr. H will teach you about change."

Mr. H asked the class to wave goodbye to Miss Quick.

After Miss Quick had left, then Mr. H asked everyone in the class to look outside the classroom windows.

The students all got out of their seats and went to the windows.

"What weather season is it outside?" asked Mr. H.

Everyone shouted their answers at the same time. Some of the students were pointing, and some moving their arms like the tree branches they saw outside, and some just very happy to be out of their seats.

Mr. H got them all to be quiet, then he asked "How fast does weather change?"

Aiden raised his hand, and Mr. H picked him to answer.

Aiden answered, "The weather does not change as fast as Miss Quick changes." Everyone in the class looked at each other and nodded their heads to agree with Aiden.

"That is right, Aiden. The weather changes more slowly." Mr. H said.

Mr. H looked at everyone in the class. He smiled at them because he knew they were going to learn something new, something different. He spoke slowly and carefully "Tomorrow we will have some fun with how fast or how slow something changes. We will call it rate-of-change or ROC for short."

"Class, for tomorrow I want each one of you to think about something very FAST and something very SLOW." said Mr. H.

"Bring two pieces of paper with you tomorrow." Mr. H told the class.

Mr. H told everyone to draw something that is very FAST on one piece of paper and something that is very SLOW on the other piece of paper.

"BBBRRRINNGGG" went the school bell for the end of the school day. Everyone rushed out of the classroom to get back home.

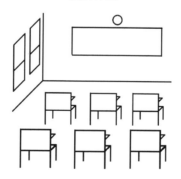

Aiden went home thinking about rate of change, ROC, and in his dreams that night sometimes he ran very FAST and sometimes he walked very SLOW and sometimes he floated high in the sky on a cloud.

2. ROC n ROL

With Blake

By

Wes Fulton

Number 2 of 26 in Series

ROC n ROL

Day-End Stories

By

Wes Fulton

Blake was Aiden's best friend.

Blake did the same school homework as Aiden, because he was also in Mr. H's class.

That day at school Mr. H asked everyone in his class if they had drawn their two homework pictures. He reminded them that one of the pictures was supposed to be about something very FAST and the other one about something very SLOW.

All the students said "Yes."

"Make sure to print your name on the back of each of your pictures." said Mr. H. Then he opened a window to let in some fresh air.

While Mr. H. was opening the window, everyone made sure they had printed their name on the back of both of their homework pictures.

"Everyone put your FAST pictures over below the windows."
Mr. H said.

The students put their FAST pictures over by and below the windows.

Some of the FAST pictures had jets and falcons and lightning bolts.

"Now, everybody, put your SLOW pictures by me." said Mr. H.

Some of the SLOW pictures had turtles and snails and jars of molasses.

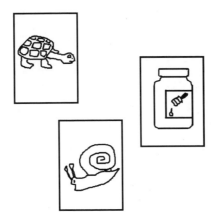

Mr. H looked at the SLOW pictures first and laughed.

"Somebody has drawn a picture of me!" Mr. H said and he smiled.

Mr. H looked on the back of the SLOW picture of himself and saw Blake's name printed.

"Blake, you are correct. I am slower than you are for sure." said Mr. H.

The whole class laughed, and Blake was embarrassed, but he smiled anyway.

"Very good picture, Blake. It does look like me." Mr. H said. Then he put Blake's SLOW picture together with all the other SLOW pictures on the board in front of the class.

Mr. H said "Class, I want each one of you to paste a star on the SLOW picture you like the best."

All the students got up from their desks and went over to the board in the front of the room to paste their star on the SLOW picture they like the best.

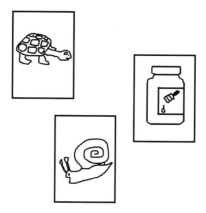

Blake's SLOW drawing of Mr. H got the most stars pasted on it. Blake smiled again.

Mr. H took the drawings of SLOW things down off the board and then put the drawings of FAST things up on the board in the front of the room.

There were drawings of cheetahs and sports cars and rockets and ice skaters among the FAST pictures.

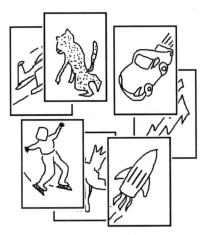

Mr. H told the class "Everyone paste a star on the FAST picture you like best."

This time it was Cora who smiled when her drawing of a lizard got the most stars.

"Cora, you did a great job in drawing a lizard. Do you have a pet lizard?" Mr. H asked.

Just then, a real lizard jumped onto Blake's head from the open window.

Blake ran around the classroom very fast with that lizard on his head.

Mr. H started to chase Blake around the classroom trying to grab that lizard off Blake's head. "I can't get the lizard if you are running so fast, Blake. Slow down so I can capture it." said Mr. H.

Blake slowed down enough so that Mr. H could grab the lizard off his head.

Mr. H put the lizard back outside the window and then closed the window, so the lizard could not get back in the classroom.

"Wow, Blake, you were running fast!" Mr. H said. "Go ahead, take a seat and rest a little."

Blake sat down and gave a big sigh of relief. Even though Blake really did like lizards, he didn't want them on his head.

Blake turned to Cora and said, "Congratulations on drawing a good-looking lizard, Cora."

Cora blushed and said, "Thank you." to Blake. "I love cute little lizards like the one that was on your head."

Mr. H asked the class "What has a higher rate of change, slow things or fast things?"

The whole class answered together "FAST THINGS!"

"So," Mr. H continued "we expect that fast things will have a higher ROC than slow things. That is natural."

Mr. H said "Everybody, don't forget to take your FAST and SLOW pictures with you. Show them to your mother or father when you get home. They might put them on the refrigerator door with a magnet to hold them."

Mr. H went over to Blake and said, "Blake with your speed, you should think about getting into sports." Blake smiled.

The school day ended just then. The classroom emptied out and the students went home.

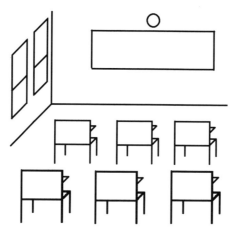

That night, Blake fell asleep dreaming about rate of change, ROC, and hundreds of cute little lizards. They all smiled at him. He ran around the room catching them one by one and putting them outside the window.

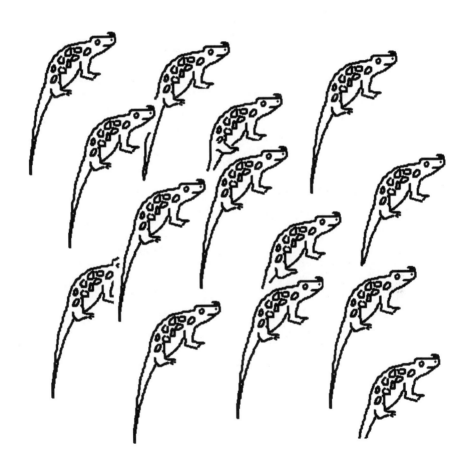

3. ROC n ROL

With Cora

By

Wes Fulton

Number 3 of 26 in Series

ROC n ROL

Day-End Stories

By

Wes Fulton

Cora liked Blake.

Cora liked Blake almost as much as she liked her cat, Sugars.

Oh, but Blake was a boy who liked to go fast almost all the time.

Cora wanted Blake to slow down and talk with her.

So, she had an idea.

When Blake ran by Cora, she tripped him and made him fall. He bruised his knee.

Blake quickly went from running very fast to being completely stopped.

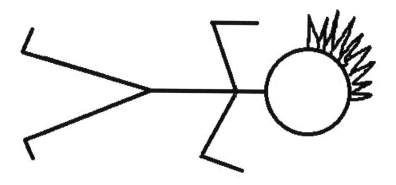

Blake got up and asked Cora "Why did you trip me? I hurt my knee!"

Cora was sorry she made Blake hurt his knee.

Cora apologized to Blake "I am sorry." and then told him "Next time, do not fall down so quickly."

Blake said to Cora "Falling down is always just as quick no matter what." Blake rubbed his knee like it was hurt badly even though the bruise on Blake's knee was very small and did not hurt much.

Their teacher, Mr. H, heard some of what was going on and came over to help Blake.

When Mr. H saw that Blake was alright and only had a very slightly bruised knee, he turned and looked directly into Cora's eyes.

Mr. H asked "Cora, did you trip Blake so that he hurt his knee?"

Cora said, "I made a mistake because I wanted Blake to slow down."

Mr. H asked, "How fast was Blake going?"

Cora said "Blake was running very fast."

Mr. H then asked Cora "Well, then how quickly did Blake stop?"

Cora said, "Blake stopped very quickly."

Mr. H said "Aha! Blake's rate of change was high. Right?" He was looking directly at Cora.

Cora stood there looking at Mr. H like he was a flea on her cat, Sugars.

"His ROC was a large value, right?" asked Mr. H again.

Cora just shook her head like she had no idea what Mr. H was asking.

"What is a ROC?" asked Cora.

"ROC stands for rate of change like we have been talking about." said Mr. H.

"Is rate of change about coins rolling down a hill?" asked Cora. She imagined someone getting change for their money, then dropping the coins by accident with the coins rolling downhill quickly.

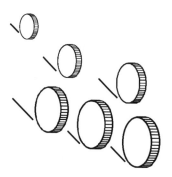

"No, the rate of change, I call it ROC for short, measures how fast something is changing." Mr. H said. "But the coin thing was a good guess."

Cora smiled and asked Mr. H "Does my cat have a ROC?"

Mr. H laughed. He replied, "Your cat was once a kitten, okay?"

Cora smiled when she thought of her little kitten that was now a cat.

"How long did it take for your kitten to change into a cat?" asked Mr. H.

Cora said that it seemed that her kitten changed into a cat quickly, but it did take weeks so maybe the change was not so quick.

Mr. H asked Cora whether Blake went from running quickly to laying on the ground faster than Cora's kitten changed into a cat.

Cora said to Mr. H "Oh yes! Blake went down to the ground quicker."

"Your kitten had a smaller ROC than Blake." said Mr. H. "The rate of change for your kitten becoming a cat was very small for a long time. Blake's ROC was very large for a short time."

Cora had already forgotten about Blake and now she was thinking about the ROC of her kitten turning into a cat.

Cora went to sleep quickly after dinner, and she dreamed about kittens changing into cats and then cats changing into piano players with their own internet videos.

4. ROC n ROL

With Davella

By

Wes Fulton

Number 4 of 26 in Series

ROC n ROL

Day-End Stories

By

Wes Fulton

Aiden liked to hang out with Davella.

Davella was a few years older than Aiden, but even so she seemed like a cool friend to Aiden.

She rode a horse on Saturdays.

Davella knew which movies were the most fun and which movies were the most scary to watch.

She played all the latest video games.

Davella told Aiden funny jokes.

She also helped Aiden with his math.

Davella was Aiden's math tutor.

Most of all Aiden liked Davella because of her father.

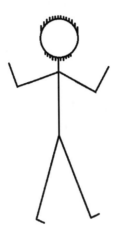

Davella's father had a special room for watching sports.

Davella wanted to teach Aiden about math in sports.

Davella invited Aiden to watch basketball in her father's sports room.

Aiden loved sports and came over to her house right away.

They got some sports-watching snacks, some popcorn and some chocolate covered peanuts, and took them into the sports room.

Davella's father had lots of pictures of famous athletes on the walls of his sports room.

There were some awesome-looking sports jerseys also on display in the sports room of Davella's father.

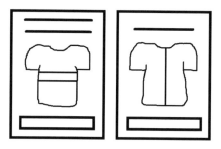

Davella turned on the television and changed the channel to the station showing the basketball game they wanted to watch.

Aiden liked to watch sports almost as much as he liked to play sports.

The favorite college team of Davella's father began to play against the team from the other side of town.

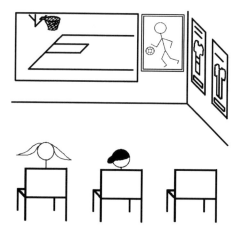

Davella's father came into his sports room wearing colored face paint representing the colors of his favorite college team. He sat down in his favorite chair next to Aiden.

Davella whispered to Aiden that her father looked silly, but Aiden was having too much fun to care about her father's looks.

Davella's father was upset about the score in the game. His favorite team was behind the other team by 5 points.

After 4 more minutes of play, his favorite team was 3 points in front of the other team.

Davella's father jumped up and started dancing.

"Why are you dancing?" Aiden asked Davella's father.

Davella's father said, "I'm dancing because my favorite team changed the score by adding 8 points more than the other team in the last 4 minutes."

Davella's father got tired of dancing very soon and sat back down in his chair.

Davella saw her chance to talk about ROC. She asked Aiden "What rate of change is that?"

Aiden was startled by Davella's question in the middle of game-watching. Aiden turned to Davella and said "What?" Then Davella's father laughed and said, "It is something you will come to expect when you are older."

Davella was still waiting. "The rate of change, the ROC, is what I want you to tell me, Aiden." she said.

"Do you mean the 8 points in 4 minutes?" asked Aiden.

"Yes, you are right Aiden! You got the correct answer." Davella said.

Aiden looked as confused as ever. "I got what correct answer?" Aiden asked.

Davella looked disappointed. "It's okay. We will talk about it later." she said. "Pass the peanuts."

Aiden passed Davella the peanuts, and they finished watching the game together.

Davella's father yelled "Yeah!" at the end of the game when his favorite team won, but he didn't dance anymore after seeing Davella give him a dirty look.

Aiden thanked Davella for inviting him, and he went home. He tossed and turned in bed that night dreaming about the rate of change and ROC and 8 points and 4 minutes. Just before he woke up, Aiden was on the basketball court dribbling the ball in a tie game between the robots of planet X and his home-base team, the Human Beans on earth. He was taking the last shot with 1 second left in the game when his alarm clock went off and he woke up from his dream. The night had gone quickly with dreaming. It was morning already and time to get ready for school.

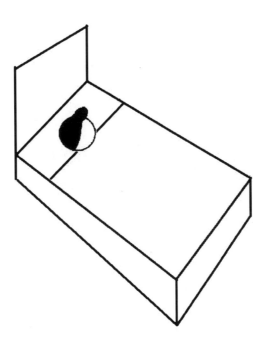

5. ROC n ROL

With Emma

By

Wes Fulton

Number 5 of 26 in Series

ROC n ROL

Day-End Stories

By

Wes Fulton

Emma rode the school bus to get to her school every day.

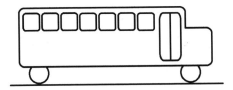

Along the way Emma noticed construction workers who were working on the road.

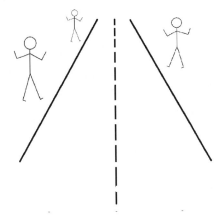

She watched giant trucks adding new road material on top of the old road.

Then other monster-sized trucks came along with huge rollers to flatten the top of the road.

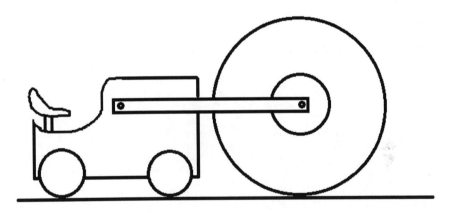

Emma thought about how big a pizza could be, if you could roll out the dough with one of those huge rollers on one of those giant trucks.

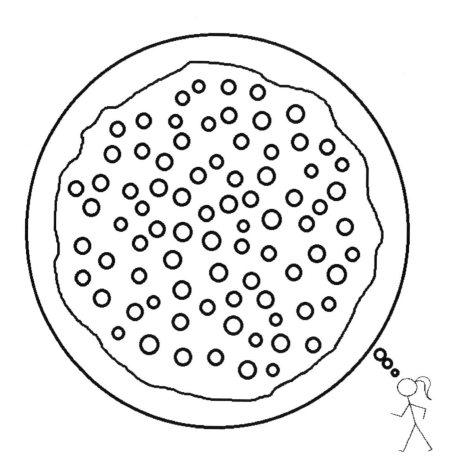

Emma was imagining the taste of a great big pizza slice as big as a house when Cora tapped her on her shoulder. Cora said "Hi."

Cora went to the same school as Emma. She was in Mr. H's class with Emma and she rode on the same bus.

"Do you have a cat in your house?" Cora asked Emma. "I like cats." said Cora.

Emma said "No, we sneeze a lot when cats are close to us. We are allergic to them."

"We do have cute little gerbils." Emma said. She was very proud of her gerbils.

"Well, we cannot have gerbils because our cat would just eat them." Cora said disappointed.

"Maybe you could rub some liver on the gerbils." said Emma.

Emma thought that liver tasted awful, and she expected everybody and everything to hate eating liver.

Emma did not know this, but many people and animals like to eat liver, especially cats.

Cats really like the taste of liver, so liver-flavored gerbils might be especially tasty to a cat.

"No, I better not put liver or any other thing on any gerbils." said Cora thinking about the last punishment she got for putting food on her cat.

"You can visit my gerbils anytime, if you leave your cat at home." Emma said to Cora.

Cora said "Thanks." as the school bus rumbled along toward school.

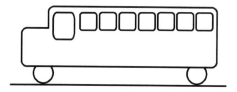

Emma looked out of the bus window at the work crew again. The workers had completed another 10 blocks of new road construction since the day before.

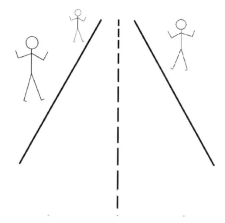

Emma saw out of the bus window that the bright orange safety cones to keep the road workers safe were moved 10 blocks further down the road than the day before.

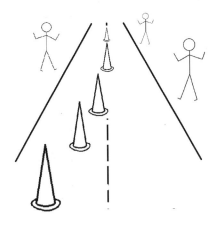

She had heard about rate of change from her teacher, Mr. H, and wanted to guess the work crew's ROC for the construction work.

"The ROC looks high for the location of the road repair work crew." Emma said to Cora trying to sound sure of herself.

Cora looked at where the work crew was and compared it to where they were yesterday.

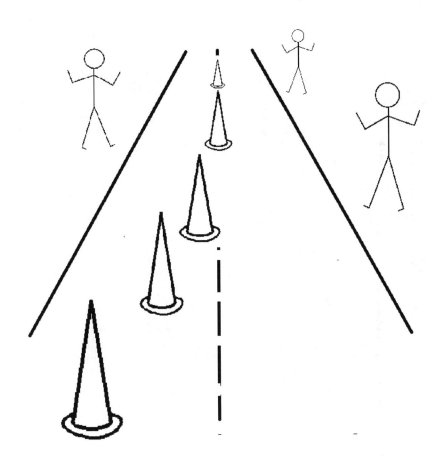

Cora said, "A rate of change of 10 blocks per day is pretty high alright." which surprised Emma.

Cora continued "I learned how to figure the ROC from Mr. H."

Cora said "You divide the amount of change difference by how long it took to make the change. That gives you the ROC for changes with respect to time."

Emma wanted to impress Cora, but Cora impressed Emma instead.

"Wow." said Emma. "Tell me again how to figure the ROC, please."

"Divide the change by how long it took to change. That is Mr. H's rate of change." said Cora.

Emma liked it because it was simple.

Just then, a motorcycle went by the bus weaving in and out of the bright orange safety cones and making a lot of noise.

Emma noticed the quick change in noise level. She looked at Cora and then thought to herself that the ROC for motorcycle noise was also high, very high, but she decided not to ask Cora about it.

That night after her dinner, Emma got sleepier and sleepier thinking about motorcycles and safety cones and rate of change. She dreamed about ice cream cones filled with candies shaped like little motorcycles.

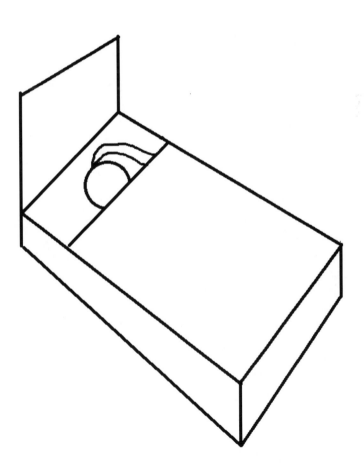

6. ROC n ROL

With Fred

By

Wes Fulton

Number 6 of 26 in Series

ROC n ROL

Day-End Stories

By

Wes Fulton

Fast-looking sports shoes always got Fred's attention.

Fred always wore fast-looking sports shoes with many spots of many colors to school. He was always happy in school wearing his favorite shoes.

He liked to put colorful shoe laces in his shoes too.

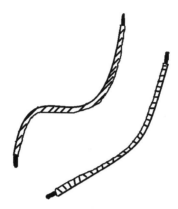

One morning Fred could not find his favorite spotted sports shoes with the colorful laces.

He looked high and low and here and there. He still could not find his favorite shoes.

Fred asked his mother "Where are my favorite sports shoes?"

"Oh, little buddy, I'm washing them now." His mother said. "They were so dirty, they almost starting walking by themselves."

Fred knew his mother was just kidding, because he had never seen or heard of any shoes walking by themselves even if they were dirty.

"Just wear some other shoes to school today." his mother said.

Even though Fred was not happy about it, he wore another pair of shoes to school. Those shoes did not have spots and did not have colorful laces.

He felt strange as he walked to school.

Fred felt that the girls waiting at the corner for the bus gave him a funny look when he walked by them.

Those girls were in his class. Fred just knew that the girls were giggling and making fun of him and his weird shoes.

Fred gave a nasty look to the girls and kept walking.

When he was in the main school hallway, Fred saw a new boy in his class who always wore a watch. That boy looked like he was staring at Fred as both boys entered Mr. H's classroom.

Fred stared back at the boy with the watch and shook his head trying to look cool. But he did not feel cool in his awful shoes.

In class Fred was distracted and not paying attention to his teacher, because he was sure that everyone was looking at him.

Fred's teacher, Mr. H, started talking again about rate of change. He asked Fred to tell the class something that had changed recently.

Fred stood up and closed his eyes and said, "All of you already know what has changed." Then he sat back down.

Mr. H looked at the rest of the students, and they looked back at Mr. H with blank stares. Nobody knew what had changed with Fred.

"Fred, nobody seems to know what changed. Please tell us." said Mr. H.

Fred looked at the girls who were on the corner waiting for the bus before and said to them "You know what is different about me."

The girls shook their heads and all together they said, "No we do not."

Fred looked at the boy wearing the watch and said, "You know what is different about me."

The new boy wearing the watch shook his head and said, "No I do not."

Fred looked even angrier than before. He decided to say what it was. He said, "All of you know that I am not wearing my favorite spotted sports shoes with the colorful shoe laces."

One of the girls who was waiting on the corner for the bus earlier said "We just noticed that you were mad. We wondered why you were not happy as you usually are, and then you gave us a nasty look."

The new boy wearing the watch said "I was surprised too when I saw you with an angry look on your face. That's all."

Mr. H stood up and said "Fred, nobody noticed your change of shoes. But everybody is noticing your change from happy to angry."

Fred thought about it and said, "I guess what I am wearing is not as important to others as I thought before."

"That is right." said Mr. H and within a quick second, Fred changed from mad to glad.

"Fred, that was a quick change from mad to glad" Mr. H said. "Now class, was that a big rate of change or a small rate of change?"

The entire class said "BIG!" all at the same time.

"That is right, class." Mr. H said. "That was a big ROC because it happened in a short time."

"Rate of change doesn't have to be over time, like ROC can be over the amount of an ingredient in a recipe. Food taste changes with amount of salt sprinkled on it. There are no limits, once you learn ROC" Mr. H said and was finished for the day.

Later after Fred was fed some red bread, he wanted to play with his friends Ned and Ted, but he read a book instead and while Fred was in his bed his eyelids felt like lead so he was ready to rest his head during the long night ahead.

As his eyelids were closing, he could not help thinking back on his big ROC day.

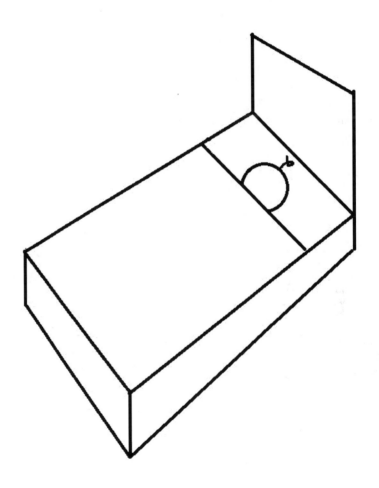

7. ROC n ROL

With Grace

By

Wes Fulton

Number 7 of 26 in Series

ROC n ROL

Day-End Stories

By

Wes Fulton

Grace sat in the back of the room in Mr. H's class.

Grace was very shy unless she was talking about her evil brother or her no-good sister. At least that is how she thought about them.

It seemed to her that her little brother played tricks on Grace whenever he could. Her older sister never paid much attention to Grace and so Grace thought her older sister was "no-good".

Grace was mostly upset with her evil brother.

Once he put a frog in her doll house. It took Grace several hours to clean her doll house after that.

Yesterday, Grace found her best doll in the garbage at her house. She had to take it out and clean it off.

She knew her evil brother had put her best doll in the garbage, because he always did stuff like that.

Grace was very fond of her dolls and did not like it when something bad happened to one of them. She started thinking about how to get even with her brother.

Just then Mr. H said "Grace, it is your turn to tell the class something about ROC." Grace remembered that she was still in class and sat up straighter.

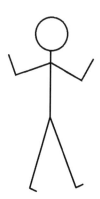

Then, Grace stood up. "Huh?" was all Grace could say. She had to stop thinking about her evil brother messing with her best doll and start thinking about Mr. H's question.

"You know, ROC, it's the rate of change. Grace, can you think of something that changes?" Mr. H asked.

"My dolls change." answered Grace.

"Really?" Mr. H responded. "How do they change?"

Grace gulped and did not say anything for a few seconds. She was very embarrassed when she had to speak especially in front of the class.

After what seemed to the class to be a long time, Grace finally said "Well, I meant to say that I change my dolls."

"Oh." Mr. H said. "You put clean diapers on your dolls. Is that right?" he asked.

Grace squirmed a little and said "No, not that."

"Okay, Grace, this is getting interesting. Tell us more." Mr. H said.

"Well, I get a new doll every year. They are new to me anyway. Some of them come from the thrift store." said Grace.

"I get some things from the thrift store myself." said Mr. H. "Go ahead and keep telling us about your dolls."

"The boys here don't want to hear anything about dolls anyway." said Grace trying to get out of talking.

"The boys in the class will all spend next class putting clean diapers on dolls if they don't pay attention." Mr. H said pointing to each one of the boys one at a time.

The boys looked at each other, and all of them straightened up, and all of them tried to look like they were really interested in what Grace was saying.

Grace felt better and said, "Every year my new doll is 3 inches bigger than the doll from the year before."

Mr. H went over closer to Grace and said, "Now we have something."

"We do?" asked Grace, and then she straightened up even more.

"The rate of change, ROC, for your dolls is 3 inches of increase each year. See how easy that is?" Mr. H asked.

Grace was now very happy to have her doll's ROC value. She felt much better about talking. She asked Mr. H "Now do you want me to tell you what my evil brother did to my best doll?"

"Ah, well, maybe we have had enough about dolls for today." Mr. H said with a smile. "Thank you, Grace, for sharing."

Later when Grace was going home after school, she stopped thinking about ROC and started thinking about her evil brother.

As soon as she got home, Grace was met at the front door by her mother.

"Grace, honey, I heard about your best doll being in the trash basket. It was my fault; I shouldn't have put it on the top of the washing machine." her mother said.

"Your doll fell into the trash basket during the regular clothes wash." said her mother.

Grace was shocked. She had been so sure that it was her evil brother who did it, but her brother did not do it. It was an accident instead.

She thought that maybe her brother was not as evil as he seemed to be, and maybe her sister was better than no-good as well.

Then Grace remembered all the other times her brother pulled tricks on her. She still did not trust her brother even though he was not the one who put her doll in the trash.

That night Grace hugged her best doll close to her as she went to sleep, dreaming about her favorite doll chasing her evil brother with a broom.

8. ROC n ROL

With Haku

By

Wes Fulton

Number 8 of 26 in Series

ROC n ROL

Day-End Stories

By

Wes Fulton

"Come here, Haku." her father said.

Haku went running to her father.

Her father was standing in their driveway next to a shiny new red sports car.

"Is that our new car?" Haku asked her father.

"No, Haku, this car is not our new car." Haku's father said with a smile. "But we can ride in it."

Haku's father worked for a car-making company.

That car company made special electric power cars for people who love to drive.

Haku thought that her father's car company made better cars than any other car she ever saw.

Haku's father worked in the test laboratory at the car company.

"My company just made this new car, and it needs to be tested." said Haku's father. "We are going to test it together if you want to ride with me."

When Haku's father told her that they were going to test the new car together, Haku jumped for joy.

Haku loved to ride when her father was driving.

"Hop in!" Haku's father said.

Haku's father put Haku in the back seat of the new car and locked her seat belt so she was safe while he was driving.

She watched her father get into the driver's seat and put on his seat belt. Then he pushed a button to start the car.

"How do we test the car?" Haku asked her father.

"We are going to drive slowly, and then we are going to drive fast." Said Haku's father.

"My teacher, Mr. H, told us about fast and slow." Haku said.

"What did Mr. H tell you about fast and slow?" Asked Haku's father.

"He told us about ROC." said Haku.

Haku's father asked, "What is the meaning of ROC?"

Haku answered her father "ROC means rate of change."

"Wow!" said Haku's father. "Do you already know about rate of change?" he asked.

Haku's face turned a little more red than usual. She blushed. She liked to surprise her father with what she learned in school.

"Yes! ROC is how fast or how slow something changes." she said.

Haku's father looked at Haku in the rear-view mirror of the shiny new red sports car and smiled.

"You are very smart, Haku." Haku's father said, and then he started to drive.

First the car went slow in the neighborhood to be safe around the neighborhood kids.

"How fast are we going, Haku?" asked her father.

Haku looked at the big speed gage in front of her father, and she saw the pointer pointing to "20".

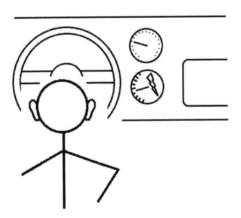

"We are going 20, Papa." Haku said.

"That's right! Now we are going to get onto the highway and go faster." said Haku's father.

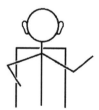

Five minutes later, Haku and her father were going fast on the highway.

"How fast are we going now, Haku?" asked her father.

Haku was starting to get sleepy. Haku looked through her sleepy eyes at the speed gage. "We are going 60 now, papa." said Haku, and then she yawned.

"We changed from 20 to 60 in 5 minutes." Haku's father said. "That is a difference of 40."

He continued "The difference in speed is the change. Now we find the rate of change, the ROC, with dividing by how long it took to make that change."

Haku didn't answer or say anything.

Her father looked in the rear-view mirror and saw that Haku was asleep. Haku's father smiled. Riding in a car always made Haku sleepy.

Haku's father drove the shiny new red car back home, took Haku out of the car and put Haku in her bed.

He kissed his smart little girl on the forehead and turned out the light and closed her bedroom door as he left. Haku was dreaming about driving a fantastic red car like the one her father was driving. Outside her room, her father could hear Haku talking and giggling in her sleep. He could not understand her words, but he could tell she was very happy.

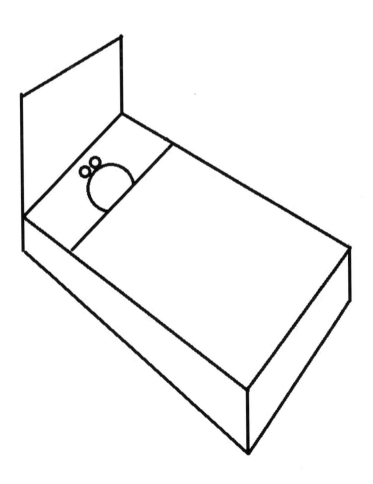

ROC n ROL

With Isidro

By

Wes Fulton

Number 9 of 26 in Series

ROC n ROL

Day-End Stories

By

Wes Fulton

Isidro was excited.

He was going to a space museum with Mr. H's class.

Isidro was hopping up and down while waiting in line at the school to get on the tour bus.

Mr. H saw that Isidro was hopping up and down.

"Isidro, why are you so excited?" asked Mr. H.

"I want to be an astronaut, and we are going to a space museum!" Isidro shouted his answer back to Mr. H even though Isidro did not actually believe he could ever become a real astronaut.

"Good answer!" Mr. H shouted back to Isidro.

The bus driver started telling everyone to get on the bus for the trip.

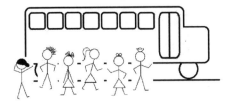

After what seemed to Isidro to be a very long wait, then everyone was on the bus.

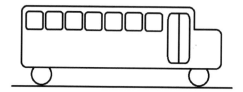

The bus driver drove the bus from the school to the space museum.

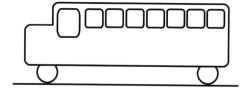

When they got to the museum, Isidro wanted to run inside, but Mr. H told everyone to be patient and wait until they were all ready to go inside.

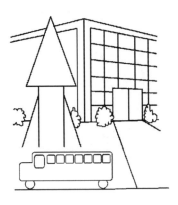

There was a giant Rocket right in front of the space museum entrance. Mr. H's class went inside together and split up into smaller groups.

Mr. H's helper, assistant teacher Miss K, took Isidro's group to the side of the lobby.

"We are going to the planetarium part of the museum first." said Miss K.

Isidro raised his hand and asked "What is a plan-tree-um? Are we going to plant some trees there?"

"Good question, Isidro. No, we are not planting trees there." said Miss K. "A planetarium makes the ceiling into a movie screen with stars and planets moving around like you would see looking up outside on a clear night."

She continued "In the planetarium, you can lean back in your chair and look up at the ceiling. It shows us how the look of the night sky changes as we move underneath it."

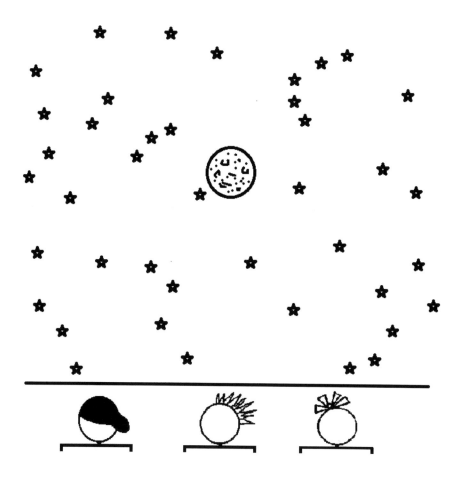

"Does it show astronauts?" asked Isidro.

"Some planetarium shows can show astronauts." said Miss K.

Now Isidro was even more excited.

Isidro wanted to be an astronaut in a planetarium show.

He wanted to build his own rocket ship with lots of rockets and lots of windows.

Isidro wanted ice cream dinners and milk shake fountains in his rocket ship.

He wanted to have a game room in his rocket ship as well.

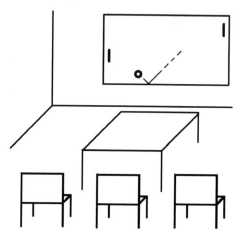

Isidro was playing video games and eating ice cream and drinking milk shakes in his rocket ship travelling through space when he heard "Isidro? Isidro?"

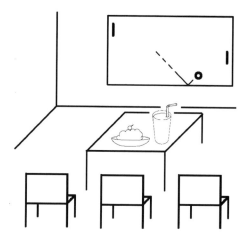

It was Miss K calling to Isidro and trying to get him to stay with her group in the space museum.

"Isidro, you were sitting in the lobby staring at the giant rocket outside." said Miss K. "Why didn't you stay with the rest of us?"

Isidro apologized to Miss K and got up to go back with the group.

Miss K stopped Isidro and grabbed his shoulder. She looked Isidro straight in the eyes.

"Were you day-dreaming about being an astronaut?" Miss K asked Isidro.

Isidro was always honest. He said "Yes, you are right. I was day-dreaming about being an astronaut, and I forgot to stay with the rest of the group."

Miss K took Isidro over to the side of the space museum lobby and sat him down. Isidro wondered how he would be punished.

"Good." Miss K said. Isidro looked completely surprised. Miss K said, "Good for you."

"You may very well become what you dream about, Isidro." said Miss K. "I dreamed about becoming a teacher, and here I am now an assistant teacher." she said.

When everyone was back on the bus to return to the school, Mr. H noticed a change in Isidro. He was not super excited and jumping around, but he was smiling.

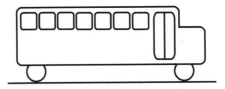

"You look different, Isidro. How do you feel?" asked Mr. H looking at Isidro's smiling face.

"I know I can become whatever I really want to be." said Isidro. Then Mr. H responded, "That is a good change at a fast rate of change, a fast ROC indeed."

Then Isidro said "Oh, and Mr. H, I almost forgot. I wrote a song about our planet." Mr. H said, "I want to hear it right now!" Isidro said, "Okay here goes."

"I live in the middle of

A little-bitty solar system

Riding on top of

A pretty blue ball.

The stars at night

They blink and they twinkle

But they look so bright

In spite of it all."

Isidro cleared his throat and said, "There's two more verses.", and Mr. H said "You are doing great, keep going."

"All I know is

I have to give a THANK YOU

To a spirit we share

Among us all.

When I think about

All my blessings

I want to hug

My pretty blue ball."

It was Mr. H's turn to clear his throat. "Just WOW, Isidro. You are going to be good at whatever you really want." said Mr. H. Then Mr. H turned around. Isidro couldn't see his face, but it looked to Isidro like Mr. H was wiping something from his eyes.

After his fast ROC day, Isidro had no problem falling asleep that night with dreams about starring in a space movie adventure as a heroic astronaut fighting off space aliens while drinking a milk shake.

10. ROC n ROL

With John

By

Wes Fulton

Number 10 of 26 in Series

ROC n ROL

Day-End Stories

By

Wes Fulton

What does John know ...

... that others don't think John knows?

Is it how to throw a curve ball?

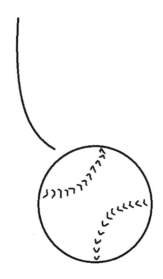

Is it how to grow bell peppers?

Is it which video game is the best to play?

Is it when to go fishing for catfish?

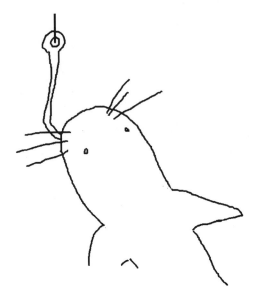

Well, John might know about some of those things but here is the surprise ...

... John knows about helping people when they are sick or when they are hurt.

John's mother is a nurse.

John's mother works in People Hospital.

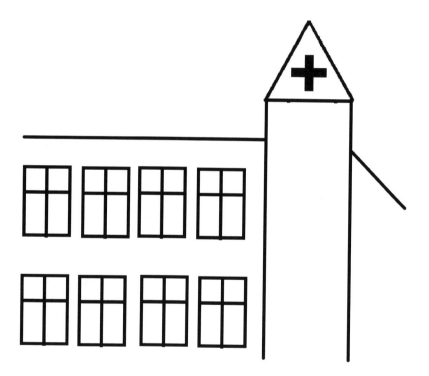

She helps people get well slowly and ...

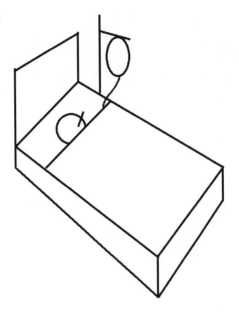

... she helps people get well quickly.

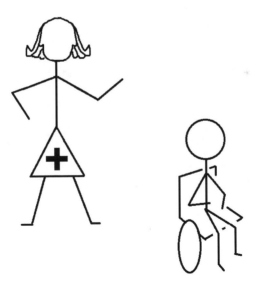

John's mother sees the rate of change in their health. The ROC is either slow or fast.

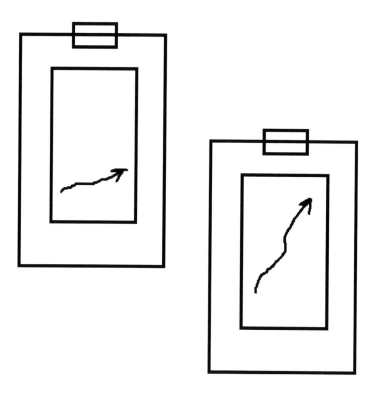

John likes to go with his mother to the hospital at visiting time. John sees lots of new things where his mother works.

He saw the laboratory room where they put tissue samples from patients onto tiny glass slides. There they use a microscope to look at the glass slides for anything strange.

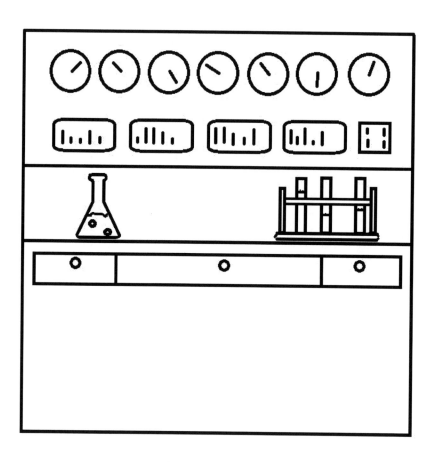

John saw the X-ray room where the doctors take bone pictures.

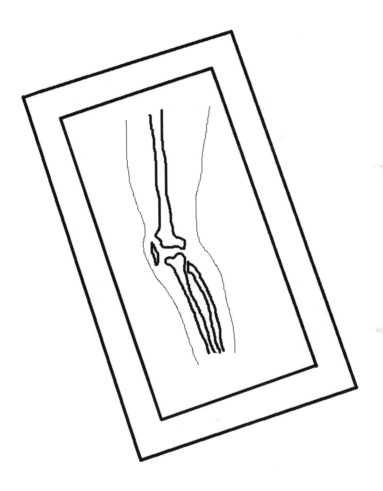

He saw the room where people exercise to get better after an operation.

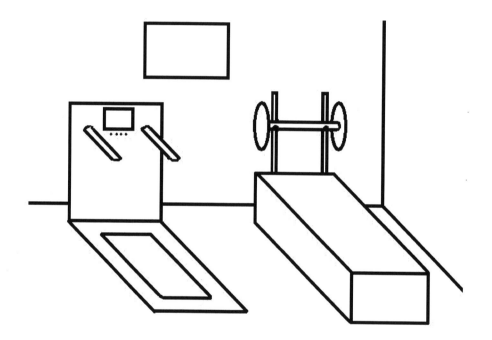

John saw the operating room where people have operations.

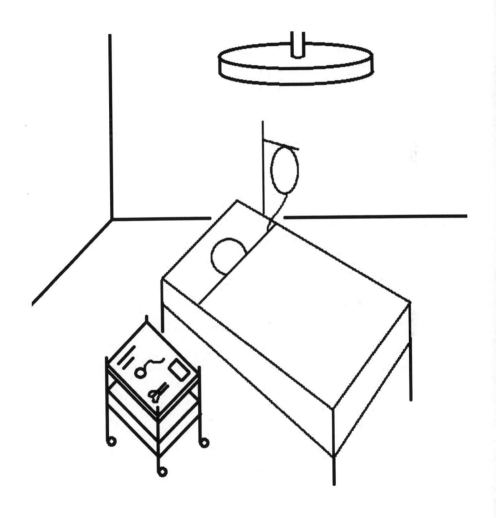

He asked his mother "What is an operation?"

John's mother likes it when John asks questions.

His mother asked him "Why do you want to know about operations?"

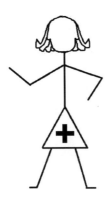

"I saw the room where people have operations." answered John.

"Oh." John's mother said. "So now you want to know what happens in that room, right?"

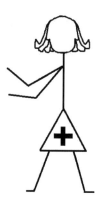

John nodded his head up and down and said "Yes."

"People go into the operating room to get big help with their sickness or their injury." said John's mother.

John's mother continued "The doctors in the operating room put the sick person to sleep first."

"When the sick person is asleep, then the doctors fix them." John's mother said to him.

"Do the doctors use hammers and saws and screwdrivers when they fix somebody?" John asked his mother.

John's mother laughed. She answered, "All the doctors have beautiful clean shiny instruments to use when they are operating on the sleeping person."

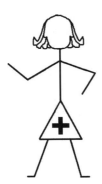

"Now do you know what happens in an operating room?" asked John's mother.

John thought for a few seconds and then said "Yes, I know about operating rooms now."

The next day when John was back in school in Mr. H's class, he noticed that Mr. H had just cut his finger.

John always kept a band aid and some clean ointment in a clear bag in his back pack just in case there was a cut. He took out the band aid and the ointment for Mr. H.

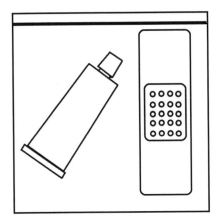

"Mr. H, put this band aid and ointment on your cut." said John.

Mr. H applied the ointment and then put the band aid on his cut.

"I feel better now. Sometimes the rate of change from feeling bad to feeling good is slow, but for me today it was very fast." said Mr. H.

Mr. H smiled. "Thank you, John. You made my ROC very fast from being cut to feeling better." he said.

John felt good every time he helped somebody.

He went home after school to find his mother wearing her coat with her car keys in her hands. "Do you want to go out for dinner tonight?" she asked.

John said "Yeah, mom that would be great!", and he and his mother went to their favorite restaurant close to the hospital, and John ate all he could eat.

John fell asleep quickly that night. He dreamed about thousands and thousands of plates of delicious food being brought to him on carts with no end in sight.

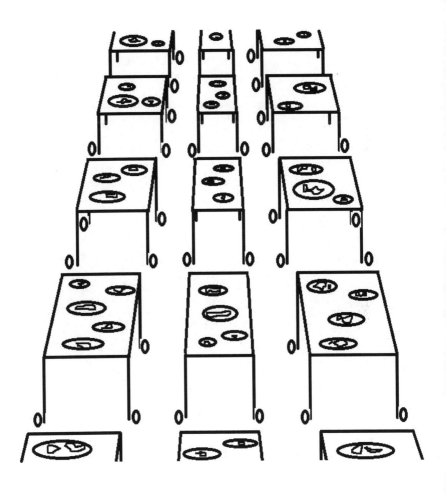

11. ROC n ROL

With Kaito

By

Wes Fulton

Number 11 of 26 in Series

ROC n ROL

Day-End Stories

By

Wes Fulton

Kaito walked a lot.

Kaito wore a leg brace, and he used a walking stick to help himself when he was going up and down hills.

He loved walking and seeing new things he passed along the way.

Kaito would walk slowly sometimes to see things better.

He walked quickly sometimes to get more exercise.

Kaito was walking uphill on the side of a road near his house when he remembered what his teacher, Mr. H, told the class yesterday.

He stopped walking for a minute to try and remember what Mr. H said.

"Everything has a rate of change. Even something that does not change has a ROC." said Mr. H.

When Mr. G said that about "no change", Kaito stood up and raised his hand.

"Kaito, you raised you hand. Do you have a question?" Mr. H asked.

"Yes, Mr. H, if something does not change then how can it have a rate of change?" asked Kaito.

Mr. H replied to Kaito's question "I can see by your question that you are paying attention. Very good, Kaito."

"The ROC for something that does not change is zero." answered Mr. H.

The next day Kaito was still thinking about Mr. H's "no change" answer as he was walking uphill.

"This road is hilly." Kaito thought to himself. "The ROC for this road is not zero."

Kaito kept walking and came to a stream with its water flowing quickly from his left to his right.

He wanted to cross the stream to continue walking uphill on the other side of it.

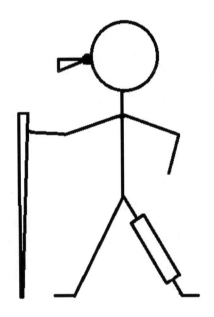

Kaito saw a flat level bridge that went above the stream from one side to the other side.

He started to walk across the flat level bridge.

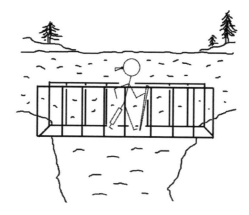

As Kaito was walking across the flat bridge he knew that he was not going up, but he was not going down either. Just then he knew what Mr. H was talking about before.

The next day in school, he told Mr. H about his walk on the bridge and that while he was on the bridge, he had an ROC of zero for how high he was.

"That is super good, Kaito." Mr. H said. "Now, going uphill, what was the ROC of how high you were?" he asked Kaito.

Kaito smiled. He thought he knew the answer but wanted to be sure first before answering.

"Could you remind me how I find the ROC when I walk uphill, please?" asked Kaito.

"You keep asking good questions, Kaito." said Mr. H.

"The rate of change only takes two numbers." Mr. H said.

"What is the first number?" asked Kaito.

Mr. H answered, "The first number you need for ROC is the amount of change or the amount of difference."

"The change in how high I was?" asked Kaito.

"Yes, that is right, first you start with the change in how high from start to finish of your climb." Mr. H said.

Kaito thought about this, and then he knew. He had started at his house and finished on top of the hill.

The top of the hill was 300 stair steps above his house.

"I went 300 stair steps up from my house. So the change from start to finish was 300 stair steps." Kaito told Mr. H.

"Excellent!" Mr. H said, and he smiled and gave Kaito a thumbs-up sign for doing a good job in knowing the difference.

Kaito felt good, but still he wanted to know the second number Mr. H mentioned.

"You said there was a second number." Said Kaito.

"Oh yes." Mr. H said. "We start with the first number which is the amount of change. Now when change is over time, the second number needed is how much time it took for the change."

Kaito remembered that it took 10 minutes. "It took 10 minutes." said Kaito.

"300 steps in 10 minutes gives ROC of 30 steps per minute. You divide the change by the time it took to make the change. That is all there is to ROC." Mr. H said.

Kaito smiled, and Mr. H said "You are learning something very powerful, Kaito. You might use this to design a rocket for Isidro."

Kaito remembered how much Isidro wanted to be an astronaut with his own rocket. That night Kaito had dreams about being in a space launch mission control room with a super gigantic big screen picture of astronaut Isidro eating ice cream while he was blasting off in his very own rocket ship.

12. ROC n ROL

With Lakeesha

By

Wes Fulton

Number 12 of 26 in Series

ROC n ROL

Day-End Stories

By

Wes Fulton

The look of the old car surprised Lakeesha.

Lakeesha expected to see a car that looked very bad. She had told Mr. H, her teacher, at recess about working on cars with her uncle, and she also told Mr. H that they were getting a junky old car to fix very soon.

But this very old car was cute-looking. It had big beautiful fenders over the tires.

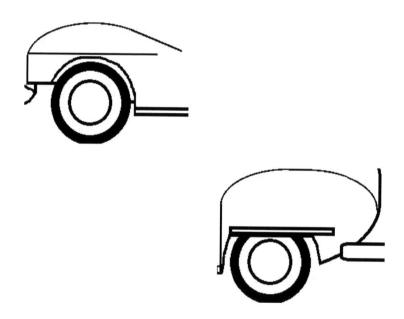

The car had large front and back and side windows.

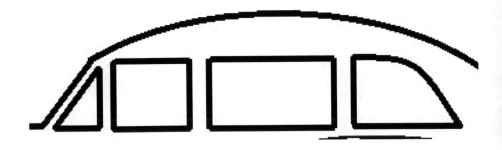

It looked to Lakeesha like someone had taken very good care of this car before her uncle bought it.

Lakeesha's uncle bought the old car yesterday so he could fix it and keep it to drive or possibly sell it to someone else.

She loved to help her uncle work on cars.

Lakeesha knew about most of the tools in her uncle's garage, and she knew their names by heart.

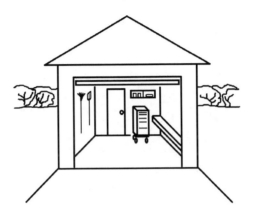

She would bring tools to her uncle from her uncle's tool box whenever he asked for them.

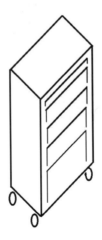

Sometimes Lakeesha helped her uncle clean and polish his cars after he finished fixing them.

Lakeesha liked the smell of a nice clean car.

Most of all, Lakeesha liked to ride in a nice clean fixed-up car.

Her uncle said, "Let's look at the engine, Lakeesha."

Lakeesha's uncle made sure that she knew about car engines.

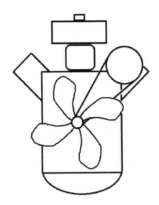

She knew that the old car's engine burned fuel to push pistons which made the crankshaft turn.

Lakeesha knew that the crankshaft in the old engine turned something along the bottom of the car to make the wheels spin.

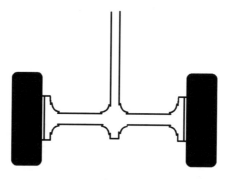

Her uncle lifted the hood of the engine compartment to look at the engine.

Lakeesha had to look at the engine too.

"Oh no!" Lakeesha said. She saw that the engine was dirty with lots of old engine oil all over.

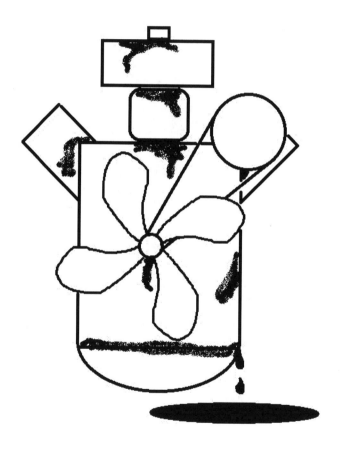

Lakeesha's uncle reached over to the engine and took a long metal stick out of it.

He showed it to Lakeesha and said, "This is a dip-stick to measure how much oil is in the engine's oil pan."

"That dip-stick also shows us how clean or dirty the oil is." Said Lakeesha's uncle.

The oil on the end of the dip-stick looked very dirty.

"We have to change the oil." said Lakeesha's uncle.

Lakeesha did not know about oil change, but she wanted to learn.

Lakeesha's uncle put a pot under the engine and then removed the engine's oil pan plug and drained the old oil into the pot. Then he put the oil pan plug back into the bottom of the oil pan.

"I am going to find out how dirty this old oil is." said Lakeesha's uncle. "I will send it out for a particle count."

"Particle count" was something new to Lakeesha, and so she decided to ask her uncle about it later.

She saw her uncle take some new cans of oil down from a high shelf and open them and pour the new oil into a tube that went down to the engine's oil pan. Then he cleaned the dipstick.

Lakeesha's uncle put the clean dipstick into the engine again. He took it out and looked at it. "That new oil has zero particle count. It is clean with no metal particles in it at all." Lakeesha's uncle said.

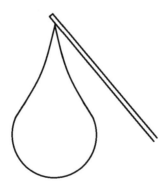

The engine started on her uncle's first try and sounded very smooth.

"The old car likes the new clean oil!" said Lakeesha. That made her uncle laugh, and he agreed with her.

"What is particle count?" she asked her uncle.

Her uncle responded "Particle count tells us how many little pieces of metal are in the oil. A smaller count means cleaner oil, and a larger count means dirtier oil."

Later the particle count report on the old oil arrived, and Lakeesha's uncle told her about it.

Lakeesha's uncle told her "The old oil had a particle count of 500 which is a lot higher than I like."

She felt very good now about the new clean oil.

Lakeesha's uncle continued "With our oil change the count went from 500 to zero, and we did it in one hour."

"The rate of change in particle count is 500 per hour in the good direction." said her uncle.

Lakeesha thought to herself "I wonder if my uncle's rate of change for particle count is the same as the ROC that Mr. H talks about in school?"

Lakeesha almost got finished telling her parents her oil change story before falling asleep that night dreaming about particle count and old funny engines that giggled when she tickled them with her uncle's tools.

13. ROC n ROL

With Manu

By

Wes Fulton

Number 13 of 26 in Series

ROC n ROL

Day-End Stories

By

Wes Fulton

Manu grew up in the countryside of India.

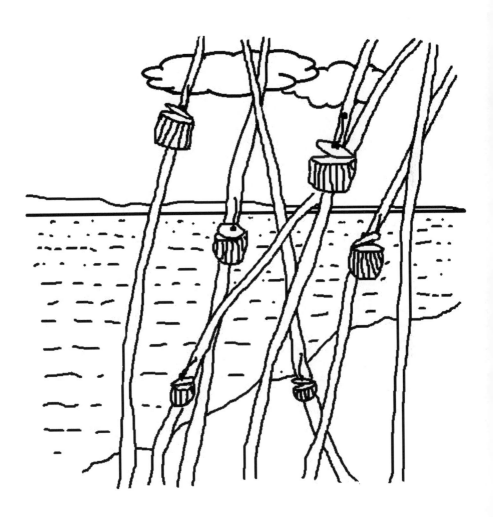

Manu remembered how he liked living among all the beautiful animals of that area. He remembered the bears and tigers of the jungle, and the cows and sheep and goats on the farms. He wanted to be an animal trainer when he grew up.

He especially liked the big friendly elephants. They used to help his family all the time with big lifting and carrying jobs.

Manu also liked where he lived now, and he enjoyed going to Mr. H's class at school.

Most of his friends were also in Mr. H's class.

Mr. H always wanted Manu to talk about where Manu used to live and all the animals that were around where Manu grew up.

One day when Mr. H was talking about rate of change, Manu had a question.

Manu raised his hand, and Mr. H said "Manu, go ahead and speak up."

Manu said "You say that the ROC or rate of change is very important. I have heard you say that many times."

"Do you have a question about the ROC, Manu?" asked Mr. H.

"Yes." said Manu and he got ready to ask his question, but he had a puzzled look on his face. Manu was not sure how to ask his question. He said "Uh …" and stopped.

Then Manu started his question again "If the rate of change is so important … ," and then he trailed off again not knowing the right way to finish his question.

"I think I got your meaning, Manu." Mr. H tried to finish Manu's thought. "You are wondering why you do not hear about ROC outside of my class if it is so important. Is that right?" asked Mr. H.

"Wow!" thought Manu to himself. "Mr. H was able to guess exactly the question I had."

Manu smiled and said "Yes, that is my question Mr. H." and he sat down with the rest of the class.

"Class, Manu has noticed something strange that not too many other people have noticed." Mr. H said.

"Students in other classes don't talk to you about ROC. You do not hear much about rate of change outside of this classroom, do you?" he asked. Mr. H looked around at all the students in the classroom.

Nobody tried to answer Mr. H's question. He was right. Nobody had heard much of anything at all about ROC outside of his class.

"Okay, I will tell you a little secret." Mr. H said.

Now some of Mr. H's students moved a little in their seats. Some of them thought they might have been selected for a secret mission.

Mr. H continued "You, each one you, are very special. You are in my class for a reason."

Now a lot of Mr. H's students started thinking that they were being punished for something they did before, and they tried thinking about what they did wrong and the possibility that they were caught doing it.

"Are you ready?" asked Mr. H.

Some of the students started thinking that maybe they were not as smart as the other students at the school, and Mr. H's class was for dummies.

"Brace yourself." said Mr. H.

By this time all the students badly wanted Mr. H to stop beating around the bush, avoiding the truth, and just tell them. Although, there were a few that thought maybe Mr. H was a space alien from another planet who came to this planet in a flying saucer.

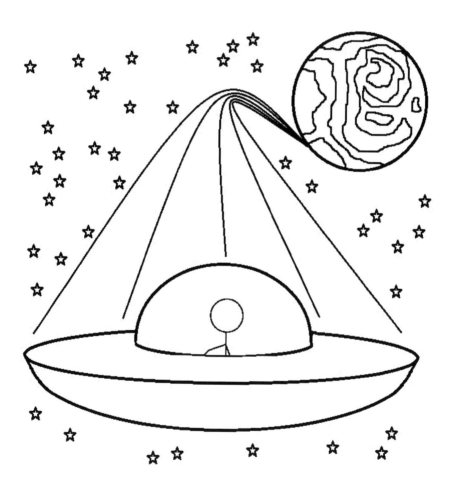

Mr. H stepped back a little and said, "I see that some of you look concerned and confused."

Manu was the one who finally got up enough courage to ask Mr. H the question that everybody had. He asked him "Mr. H, why don't you just tell us the answer?"

"Do all of you want to know why?" asked Mr. H.

All the students said together "YES ... WE ALL WANT TO KNOW WHY!"

"That's right. You all want to know why. That is the reason all of you are in my class." said Mr. H.

At this point every single student in Mr. H's class was totally confused. Nobody thought Mr. H was making any sense. Now they were all thinking that Mr. H might just be crazy.

Mr. H explained "All of you are curious, and you want to know why and how and where and when and what. Not everybody is so lucky to have your questions."

"For some people it is enough just to see the rainbow. For others, like all of you in my class, you want to see the rainbow ... AND you want to know how it shines, why it shines, and what makes it so beautiful." Mr. H said.

Mr. H wasn't finished. He said, "I picked you specially to be in my class so you could learn the language of why, to be explorers on the best planet in the universe, this one."

Mr. H continued, "The language of why is math, and ROC is at the top. Rate of change is part of the highest and most powerful math."

Manu raised his hand again. "Will we learn WHAT is in the school lunch?" he asked.

Mr. H laughed and laughed. "You are right, Manu, what is in the school lunch is a big mystery." he said.

"Manu if you find out, please tell the rest of us." Mr. H said still laughing. The school bell rang "BBBRRRINNGGG" for the end of the school day.

Mr. H wrote "ROC" on the board at the front of the class. "Learn this, and you will be way ahead of everybody else your age. Now go home at get some rest." he said. All the students left to go home.

That night, Manu tried to explain Mr. H's words to his parents. They smiled at him, but he knew they didn't understand. They helped Manu into bed. He was asleep in a flash dreaming about lots of elephants in Mr. H's class asking question after question.

14. ROC n ROL

With Ning

By

Wes Fulton

Number 14 of 26 in Series

ROC n ROL

Day-End Stories

By

Wes Fulton

Every morning Ning had a good breakfast.

Ning's breakfast was not too big.

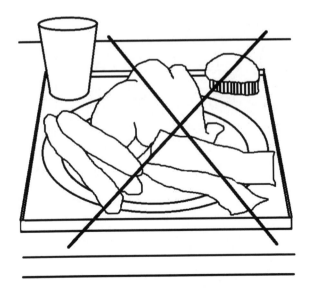

Her breakfast was not too small.

Ning thought her breakfast was just the right size.

Ning's mother made sure Ning started the day with just the right amount of nutritious food for her to be healthy and happy.

After breakfast on school days, Ning went to school.

It seemed like all her friends were in Mr. H's class at school.

Aiden and Blake and Fred and Isidro and John and Kaito and Manu were there with Ning in Mr. H's class.

Cora and Emma and Grace and Haku and Lakeesha were there with her in Mr. H's class.

Grace walked by Ning going into Mr. H's class and said "Hello."

Ning asked, "How are you doing today, Grace?"

"Okay, I guess." said Grace with a half-smile. Then Grace slowly walked over to her desk.

Grace plopped herself down into her desk chair, as if someone were putting down a heavy sack of potatoes.

Ning thought Grace looked as if she was drooping all over like wet clothes on a clothes line.

"Good morning, Mr. H." everyone said when Mr. H came into the classroom.

Everyone sat up in their chairs as Mr. H said, "Top of the morning to all of you!" Everyone except Grace.

Grace managed to shift a little in her desk, but she didn't sit very straight.

When Mr. H looked over the class, he noticed that Grace was looking tired.

Mr. H waited until recess before he talked to Grace about how tired she looked.

Grace was sitting by herself at recess when Mr. H came by to talk to her. Grace stood up slowly.

"Hey, Grace. How are you feeling?" asked Mr. H.

Grace looked up at Mr. H and said "Okay, I guess." just like she said it to Ning before.

"You look a little tired." Mr. H said. "Did you get enough sleep last night?" he asked her.

Grace said "Yes I did. I slept for 9 hours last night."

"Do you have a fever?" asked Mr. H.

Just then, Ning came running by and almost tripped over her own feet because she was running so fast. She came to a stop right by Mr. H and Grace.

"Mr. H, what are you and Grace talking about?" asked Ning.

Mr. H said "Oh nothing really, Ning. You and Grace go ahead and play until recess is over." Then, Mr. H went back into the classroom.

Grace was standing still like a park statue. Ning grabbed Grace's hand to pull her.

"I don't feel like playing." said Grace.

Ning said, "After my good breakfast, I feel like I am full of energy."

"Oh, I don't care much for breakfast." said Grace. Right then, Ning immediately knew what to do.

The next day on her way to school, Ning brought some yummy breakfast bars. Ning saw Grace before school and offered her one of the breakfast bars.

"My mother bought these at the health store. They really taste good." said Ning to Grace.

"Oh, no thank … " Grace started to say, but Ning immediately opened the breakfast bar wrapper and put the breakfast bar in Grace's hand. Ning said, "Just taste it."

Grace went ahead and started eating the breakfast bar. She decided it did taste pretty good and didn't stop eating it until it was completely gone.

In class that day, Mr. H noticed that Grace didn't look tired.

Later at recess, Mr. H went over to Grace and said, "You really changed since yesterday."

"Yes, I have a lot of energy." said Grace with a big smile.

"You got an energy boost in one day. That is a big rate of change!" said Mr. H. "Why is there such a big ROC?" he asked. "I don't know." said Grace. Then she looked at Ning and smiled and said, "I think Ning helped."

Grace went to sleep later that evening thinking about how lucky she was to have a good friend like Ning. Grace dreamed about being in a foot race with Ning on a road made from breakfast bars floating high in the sky.

15. ROC n ROL
With Olga

By

Wes Fulton

Number 15 of 26 in Series

ROC n ROL

Day-End Stories

By

Wes Fulton

Olga didn't know the answer to Mr. H's question.

Then Olga remembered that Mr. H was always talking about rate of change in class.

"It is a ROC." said Olga hoping that the true answer was something like that.

"Very good, Olga!" Mr. H said.

Olga looked around Mr. H's classroom at everybody while she was smiling a big smile just like she had solved a major world problem.

"You are right, Olga. We measure speed to see how fast something's position is changing. Speed is the ROC of position over time." said Mr. H.

"Of course. The rate of change of position would have to be speed. Everybody knows that." said Olga trying to sound really smart. She smiled her big smile again hoping the boys were paying attention.

"Olga, I think you really understand this." Mr. H said. "Okay, Olga, what is the difference in speed over time?" asked Mr. H.

Olga stopped smiling, and she started to stare at her hands.

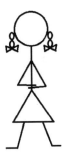

Olga took a deep breath. She looked out the window to her left. She put her chin on top of her right fist.

She hoped she looked like she was thinking deeply, like that statue about thinking by Rodin in the art museum.

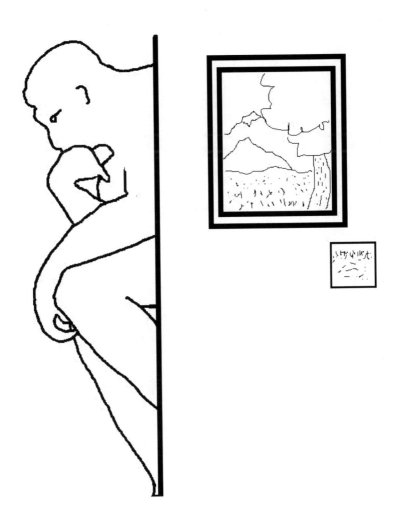

Finally, Olga gave up trying to think of the correct answer. She simply didn't know. She decided to just answer exactly the way she did before.

"It is a ROC?" her answer came out sounding like a question.

"That is right. I knew you could do it!" shouted Mr. H. Then Olga was able to smile a little after she got past the surprise of getting the right answer.

Mr. H looked around at all the students. "What do we call the ROC of speed?" he asked.

Lakeesha stood up and raised her hand, and Mr. H picked her to answer. Olga felt relieved, because Mr. H was getting someone else to answer.

"Acceleration is the ROC of speed. You use the accelerator pedal in your car to change your speed, to get acceleration." Lakeesha said and then she sat back down.

Mr. H remembered that Lakeesha told him she helped her uncle work on cars. "Terrific, Lakeesha. You should know. You help your uncle work on cars." Mr. H said.

The boys all suddenly looked over at Lakeesha like she was the latest video game.

Lakeesha didn't pay attention to the boys. She pretended that she didn't care that all the boys were looking at her.

Now Olga wondered why all the boys were not looking at her. Instead they were all looking at Lakeesha. It must be the car thing Olga thought.

Olga decided then and there that she needed to learn more about cars.

"Mr. H?" Olga asked as she raised her hand. She wanted to try to get everyone's attention back on her. "Do people have a ROC?"

Mr. H laughed. "That is one of the things that makes life fun." he said.

"Everybody changes. Some people change slowly, and other people change very quickly." Mr. H said.

Mr. H continued "Young people usually have a big ROC, and old people mostly have a small ROC."

Olga knew her own rate of change was big. It seemed like she was changing every day.

When it was time to go home from school, Olga wanted to stay and talk to Lakeesha.

She saw Lakeesha walking by the school cafeteria.

"Lakeesha!." shouted Olga to get her attention. Lakeesha turned around to face Olga. "Yes." said Lakeesha.

"Why does your uncle work on cars?" Olga asked Lakeesha.

Lakeesha looked at Olga and smiled. "Isn't it strange now you are interested in cars? You were never interested in cars before." she said.

Olga didn't hesitate to answer "Okay I will tell you, but you already know why. I saw everyone looking at you when they found out you work on cars with your uncle."

"Cars are fun, Olga. Do you want to help me and my uncle?" asked Lakeesha.

Olga started to like Lakeesha a lot. "Oh yes! When do we start?" asked Olga. Then Lakeesha said "Well I'll have to ask my uncle first, but maybe right away."

When Olga got home, she finished her homework and went straight to bed.

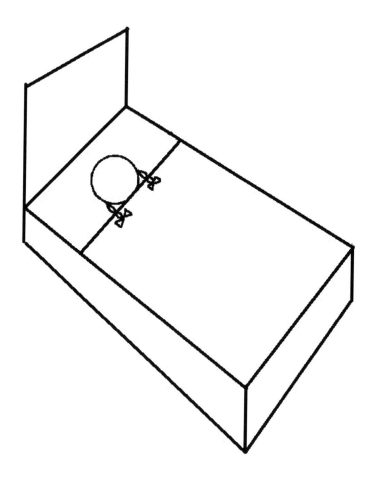

Olga's dreams that night were about her and Lakeesha. They were running their own car repair business with hundreds of old cars to repair. After they repaired a convertible, then they put the convertible top down and drove around town with their hair blowing in the breeze and with lots of boys watching them and wanting to ride with them too.

16. ROC n ROL

With Pradeep

By

Wes Fulton

Number 16 of 26 in Series

ROC n ROL

Day-End Stories

By

Wes Fulton

Just before going to bed, Pradeep looked in the bathroom mirror.

There was Pradeep looking back at him from the mirror.

Pradeep moved to the left, and so did the mirror image.

Pradeep brushed his teeth, and so did the mirror image.

Pradeep wondered "Why can't the mirror image do my homework?"

Pradeep looked at himself in the mirror and smiled. He knew the mirror image could not do his homework. The mirror image was the same image as himself.

The only way the mirror image was going to do homework is if Pradeep was in front of the mirror doing his homework.

It was already late. Pradeep went to sleep. Pradeep woke up the next morning still thinking about the mirror image.

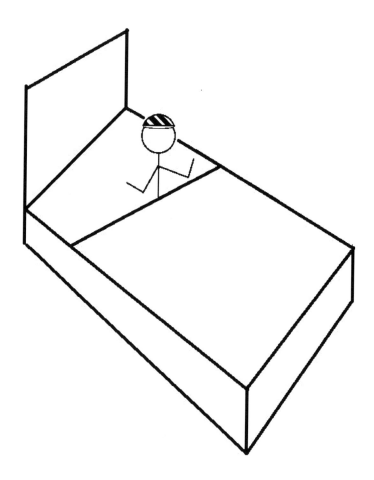

Pradeep went to school that morning thinking about how the mirror image was the same as his own image.

Pradeep went up to Mr. H at recess. "Mr. H," Pradeep said "my mirror shows the same image as mine. Why?" asked Pradeep.

Mr. H was very pleased that Pradeep was asking such a fantastic question. "Nice question." Mr. H said.

"The mirror bounces back the light that hits it" said Mr. H. "There is a coating like silver at the back of the mirror's glass."

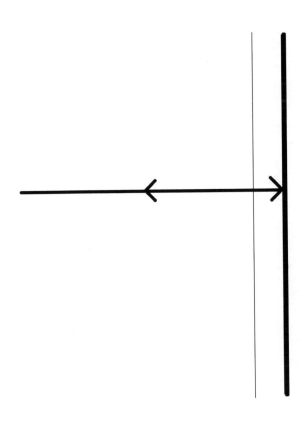

"When we are in the light and in front of the mirror, the light shining off from us hits the mirror and then bounces right back to our eyes and we see ourselves." explained Mr. H.

Mr. H added "The image we see is equal to the mirror image in front of the mirror."

"Equal?" Pradeep asked. "What is equal?"

"I'm glad you asked, Pradeep." Mr. H said and patted him on the back. "Equal is my favorite word."

Pradeep was still wondering what the word equal had to do with the mirror, when Mr. H saw something outside that could possibly help Pradeep to understand about the word equal.

Mr. H brought Pradeep over to the classroom window. "Do you see that see-saw outside there in the recess area, Pradeep?" asked Mr. H.

Pradeep looked at the see-saw out in the playground only a little bit away from the classroom windows.

"Aiden is on one side of the see-saw, and Emma is on the other side." said Mr. H.

"Yes, I see," said Pradeep "but Aiden is down and Emma is up, and they are not moving even though they are trying."

"Why is Aiden staying down and Emma staying up even though they are trying to move?" Mr. H asked.

Pradeep knew the answer to Mr. H's question. "Aiden weighs more." said Pradeep.

"You got it, Pradeep. Very good." Mr. H said. Then he asked, "If Aiden's weight was the same as Emma's weight, what would happen?"

Pradeep knew the answer to that question too. "Both sides would balance, and they could go up and go down." he said.

Mr. H went right in front of Pradeep and said "You are right again. When both weights are the same value then we say they are equal."

"If Aiden had equal weight to Emma, then it would be easy to make the see-saw go up and down." Mr. H said.

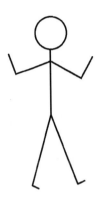

Mr. H saw that Pradeep was thinking about something. Pradeep seemed to be confused. Mr. H asked "Pradeep, are you confused about something?"

Pradeep sat down at a table in the classroom. He looked at Mr. H and asked, "How could Aiden's weight be exactly the same as Emma's weight?"

"You caught me." said Mr. H. "Aiden's weight and Emma's weight would always be at least a little different."

Mr. H continued "In science and math we use the word equal to mean that something is exactly the same as something else, but people are all at least a little different. The differences from person to person make the world interesting."

"Even though each person is special and different and one-of-a-kind, every person deserves equal treatment from the law." Mr. H said.

Pradeep had to smile. He had heard the same thing from his mother.

Pradeep stood up and said, "My mother says the equal thing as you."

At that moment, Mr. H knew that Pradeep understood about the word equal. Pradeep knew that something equals something else if their values are the same.

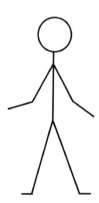

At the end of the school day, Pradeep waved goodbye to Mr. H and headed for home.

Later Pradeep got sleepy and went to bed thinking about being equal. He dreamed about two mirrors on a giant see-saw, a little mirror and a big mirror. The little mirror was down, and it was making fun of the big mirror up in the clouds that was getting all wet. The big mirror looked down at the little mirror and said "Hey, I'm supposed to be down. I am heavier than you are, and you are lighter than I am!" The little mirror laughed and said "You are in a dream silly, what do you expect?" Then the big mirror turned just right to shine the rays of the bright sun into the little mirror. The surprised little mirror fell off of the see-saw, and that brought the big mirror down. The little mirror saw its reflection in the smiling big mirror and said "Thanks, big mirror, for showing me how beautiful I am."

17. ROC n ROL

With Quon

By

Wes Fulton

Number 17 of 26 in Series

ROC n ROL

Day-End Stories

By

Wes Fulton

Quon always sat in the back of Mr. H's class.

Quon was new in the class and didn't want to draw a lot of attention to himself.

Mr. H knew that Quon was shy and only called on him to answer when Quon was sure to know the answer.

"Quon, did you do your homework?" asked Mr. H.

Mr. H knew that Quon always did his homework.

Quon stood up and answered "Yes, Mr. H."

Quon held up some pages with his writing on them.

Mr. H nodded his approval. "We had some new words to learn." Mr. H continued.

Mr. H walked over to the board and wrote 4 words, "Equal", "Equals", "Equivalent", and "Equation".

Mr. H turned to look at Quon. "Tell us about each one of those words please, Quon." said Mr. H.

Quon was sure about the answer for the first two words, but he was not as sure about the last two words.

Quon said "When something has the same value as something else, then we say they are equal."

"That is a good explanation of the word equal. What about equals, Quon?" Mr. H asked.

Quon didn't say anything right away. He was thinking about what to say that would sound best.

Finally, he said "Coming to school late equals big trouble."

Mr. H laughed and said, "Very good, Quon."

Quon asked "Mr. H, Can somebody else answer about the last two words?"

Mr. H nodded his head and said "Yes of course, Quon. Thank you. You can sit down."

After Quon sat down, Mr. H looked at Haku. She looked like she knew and appeared like she was ready to answer.

"Haku, can you tell us about the word equivalent?" asked Mr. H.

Haku stood up. "Equivalent means the same as equal." said Haku with great confidence.

"So equivalent is equal to equal, and equal is equivalent to equivalent, right?" Mr. H asked Haku while he was smiling a little to himself.

After thinking about Mr. H's answer for a few seconds, then Haku slowly nodded her approval and then sat down hoping that what he said was correct. It sounded correct to Haku.

The lunch bell went off signaling the time for lunch. Mr. H dismissed everyone for lunch.

Quon almost always brought his own lunch from home, but today his father had given him money to buy his lunch from the school cafeteria. In the cafeteria Quon sat with Haku.

Quon and Haku ate lunch quietly. Then Quon turned to Haku "Thanks for telling us about the word equivalent. I knew about equal and equals, but I wasn't sure about equivalent." said Quon. "Do you know what equation is?" Quon asked Haku.

Haku was starting to explain about equations when the bell rang to show that lunch time was over.

Haku turned to Quon and said, "I'll tell you in class about equations, if Mr. H asks me to do it." Then they left the cafeteria to return to class.

Back in class, Mr. H did ask Haku to explain the meaning of the word equation.

Haku liked to explain things. She stood up and began walking to the front of the class.

On the board, Haku wrote something. "Every equation has 3 parts." She said.

Haku continued "The first part is the left side. The second part is an equal's sign that looks like two short flat lines one above the other. The third part is the right side. So, you have left side, equals sign, right side."

Haku finished with "The equation shows that the left side and the right side have the same value, and that they are equal."

"Perfect!" said Mr. H. "One more thing about equations. Making the same change to both sides at the same time keeps the equation balanced just like a balanced see-saw so both sides stay equal, and that is all we need to know about equations."

"We have made a great step in our journey of understanding. When we combine equations with ROC, we are cooking at the highest level of math and science." Mr. H said, and with that the school day was finished.

After school, Quon and Haku talked some more. Haku said she learned something new every day in Mr. H's class. They continued talking until Quon's father came to pick him up. Quon got into his father's car and fell asleep riding home.

Quon's father moved him from the car to Quon's bed. His father took off Quon's watch from his arm and put it on the nightstand by Quon's bed. Even though Quon liked to wear his watch everywhere, his father didn't want Quon to accidentally scratch himself with it while he was sleeping. Quon dreamed that night he was on top of a tall building on a see-saw with Haku. Haku jumped hard on her side of the see-saw and Quon went flying through the clouds. He landed on top of a flying airplane and used it like a surfboard. Then he was surfing on the clouds just like surfing on ocean waves.

18. ROC n ROL

With Ringo

By

Wes Fulton

Number 18 of 26 in Series

ROC n ROL

Day-End Stories

By

Wes Fulton

Ringo never missed anything.

If anything happened somewhere around where Ringo lived, then he would always hear something about it.

He saw things that other people might easily miss.

Ringo wanted to become a detective.

He wanted to solve mysteries that other people could not solve.

Ringo's favorite books were about detectives and solving crimes. He really liked to read stories written by Sir Arthur Conan Doyle.

Ringo's teacher, Mr. H, could always find out the latest news from Ringo, because Ringo loved to collect facts and especially numbers.

This was the day that Mr. H wanted to have fun with Ringo, by asking him some strange questions in class.

"Ringo?" Mr. H asked. "Do ocean waves go up or do they go down?"

Ringo put his hands on his stomach and laughed, because he thought Mr. H's question did not make any sense.

"Mr. H," said Ringo "Ocean waves go up, then go down, then go up, then go down, over and over."

"Are you sure the ocean waves can't keep going only in one direction?" asked Mr. H.

"Ocean waves cannot keep going up all the time, and they can't keep going down all the time either." said Ringo. He had a smile on his face, because he thought Mr. H was being silly.

Mr. H wanted to have more fun with Ringo. He asked him "Why can't the waves keep going up?"

Ringo rolled his eyes and grabbed his head and looked like he was talking to a pet mouse who didn't understand anything he was saying.

"There is not enough water in the ocean for the waves to keep going up all the time." said Ringo.

Then Mr. H bent over with his hands just above the floor. "Alright, how about the ocean waves always going down … what about that?" Mr. H asked Ringo.

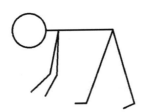

Ringo guessed that Mr. H was getting too old and not thinking very well. He wondered if anybody else had noticed it.

Ringo spoke very slowly as if he was talking to a baby "If the ocean waves kept going down all the time, then pretty soon there would be no oceans."

Ringo now wondered if he should go get the school nurse to look at Mr. H, because Mr. H was asking some very dumb questions for a teacher.

Mr. H cleared his throat "Mmmmm. Okay, then what would you call the motion of the ocean?" he asked Ringo.

"Wavy" said Ringo, then he moved his hand in a wavy motion up and down.

Mr. H asked, "If I was not moving at all, in other words if I was staying in the same place, and I was in the middle of the waves, what would that kind of motion look like to me?"

Ringo put his left arm out in front of himself pointing toward the ceiling, and then he moved his right hand back and forth on his left arm to show Mr. H what ocean wave motion would look like to someone who was not moving.

Mr. H turned away from Ringo and looked out the classroom window. Then he said, "It sure would be nice if there was an equation for wavy motion like that."

The school bell rang just then, "BBBRRRINNGGG", for the end of the school day. Mr. H said goodbye to all the students, and they left the classroom.

As Ringo was leaving school, he wondered why Mr. H asked so many weird questions about wavy motion. He decided to become a detective to find out.

Ringo rode his bicycle to the public library.

He saw a friendly lady sitting at the library entrance. "Where are your books on wavy motion?" he asked her.

"What kind of wavy motion, dear?" the friendly lady asked Ringo.

"Motion of the ocean." said Ringo. He moved his hand on his arm like he did for Mr. H.

"You are moving like a sine wave." the lady at the library entrance said. "The books on sine waves are in the math area of the library."

"Oh!" Ringo thought to himself. Now he knew why Mr. H was asking those questions that sounded silly before.

Mr. H was not completely crazy like Ringo was starting to think. Mr. H wanted Ringo to do detective work on sine waves.

Before Ringo left the library, he read 2 books on sine waves.

Ringo learned about circles, and angles and wavy motion, and up and down, and back and forth. He was amazed to find out that many of the things he already knew about had lots of sine wave motion in them.

The next day Ringo went to school knowing more about wavy motion than any of his friends in class.

Mr. H had just started the class when Ringo raised his hand. "Yes, Ringo." Mr. H said.

"It's a sine wave." said Ringo. Nobody else in the class knew what Ringo was talking about, but Mr. H knew. He smiled at Ringo and gave him a friendly royal wave with his hand.

"Our class detective, Ringo, has some information on a very important kind of ROC. It is the rate of change we call sine wave. Especially in science, that kind of motion comes up everywhere. Tell us about it, please." Mr. H said to Ringo.

Ringo held the attention of the rest of the class as he talked about vibrating guitar strings, sound waves, magnets, pulsating stars, and TV signals. Ringo slept well that night. He dreamed about a TV game show with a wavy Mr. H out in front asking crazy questions of the people playing the game.

19. ROC n ROL

With Sachi

By

Wes Fulton

Number 19 of 26 in Series

ROC n ROL

Day-End Stories

By

Wes Fulton

Sachi had too many followers.

Sachi had a hard time keeping track of so many people. There were hundreds of followers called "friends" in her social network. They followed what she did, and she followed what they did.

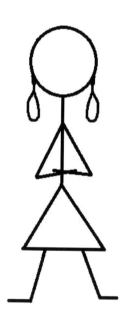

Every friend in her social network was special to Sachi, she had lots of pictures of them, and she didn't want to lose track of her friends or her pictures.

To keep track of all her social network friends, Sachi put them into groups.

Her neighborhood friends were all in one group.

Sachi's school friends were in another group, and some school friends were also her neighborhood friends.

Sachi also had her family group.

Sachi had her tennis-playing group.

There were other people in her drama group. She had people in other countries in another group.

Sachi's social network on the computer kept all the pictures of her friends and how to contact them and their birthdays and even their favorite colors, but Sachi wanted to know how the social network did all that.

In school Sachi remembered to ask her teacher, Mr. H, how the social network could keep track of all that information on all her hundreds of friends.

Mr. H said "That's a lot of information.", then he looked like he was thinking about something else for a few seconds. Finally, he said "We did it differently before computers."

"None of us could keep all the information together on hundreds of friends before computers." said Mr. H.

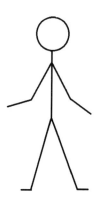

Sachi gave Mr. H a smile and wondered if he was ever going to answer her question.

Mr. H smiled back at Sachi and asked her "Do you know about arrays?"

Sachi thought Mr. H might be talking about all the rays of sunlight coming out in all directions from the sun. She even imagined a few sunspots on the sun.

"Do you mean rays of sunlight?" Sachi asked Mr. H.

"No, I wasn't thinking about that, but now I am." said Mr. H, and he put his arms in back of his head like he was laying in the sun on the beach.

Then Mr. H started to rub his upper arms. To Sachi, Mr. H looked like he was warming himself on a cold night in front of a fire. She didn't think too much about it though. Mr. H was always doing strange things.

Sachi waved her hand in front of Mr. H's face to get his attention. She asked him "Does it have something to do with laser rays?"

"No, nothing to do with laser rays that I know of, but that would be cool." said Mr. H to Sachi. He pointed his index finger out and curled the rest of his fingers into a small make-believe laser beam maker and then pretended he was aiming it at imaginary locations on the ceiling.

"Okay, I give up, tell me about the rays you were talking about." Sachi said to Mr. H.

"We call them ar-rays and they are special number groups." Mr. H said.

Mr. H continued "Numbers are put into arrays like your friends are put into special groups."

"When the numbers are grouped like your friends, then those numbers are easy to connect and easier to study." Mr. H explained.

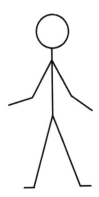

"We can even have rate of change arranged in arrays of ROC values, but let's look at a very simple example with words instead." Mr. H said.

Mr. H went over to the board and wrote words in a special pattern.

Cora	Blue
Emma	Red
Grace	Green
Haku	Red

"Is that an ar-ray?" asked Sachi.

Cora	Blue
Emma	Red
Grace	Green
Haku	Red

"Very good, Sachi." said Mr. H. "Yes, that is an array showing names of some of your friends and across from each one of them is their favorite color."

Cora	Blue
Emma	Red
Grace	Green
Haku	Red

"Those are NOT their favorite colors, Mr. H." said Sachi, because she knew all the favorite colors of her friends. She pursed her lips, put her hands on her hips, and gave Mr. H a nasty look.

Cora	Blue
Emma	Red
Grace	Green
Haku	Red

Mr. looked back at Sachi and said "Alright. Maybe those are not their real favorite colors. Let's just pretend that they are favorites for now, okay?" he asked Sachi. She slowly nodded her head to indicate that it was okay for now.

Cora	Blue
Emma	Red
Grace	Green
Haku	Red

Mr. H looked at the array on the board and said, "From the array on the board, I can see there are two people with red as their favorite color."

Cora	Blue
Emma	Red
Grace	Green
Haku	Red

"I can also tell from this array of words on the board that every friend has a different name." Mr. H said.

Cora	Blue
Emma	Red
Grace	Green
Haku	Red

Mr. H went on "This array on the board uses words. It is easier inside the computer to handle the information by using an array that represents everything with numbers. So, let's change the array to numbers." He went to the board and wrote another array.

637	58
214	13
1102	34
516	13

"Does all the information in computers look like that?" asked Sochi.

637	58
214	13
1102	34
516	13

Mr. H went back to the board bringing his calculator this time, and after using the calculator a while he wrote another different looking array on the board. "That same array in the computer would look more like this." He said.

1001111101	111010
11010110	1101
10001001110	100010
1000000100	1101

"The computer works mostly with zeroes and ones." Mr. H said. "But notice, the computer is still using some kind of array. Lots of big problems are solved on the computer with arrays."

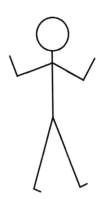

Mr. H kept talking. "Before you go home, I want you to understand that some people use different words to mean the same thing. Another name for an array is the word matrix, but it means the same thing." he said.

Sachi thanked Mr. H for teaching her about arrays.

The day had been most interesting for Sachi. She didn't understand it all, but now she had a better idea about how her social network could keep a whole lot of information together on her friends.

Sachi went to bed later and saw arrays and sun rays and laser light ray makers in her dreams. The sun rays grouped themselves by how long they were. The longer sun rays didn't want to play with the smaller ones. The smaller sun rays all had laser light ray makers and were pointing cosmic rays at the longer arrays. The longer arrays ran and hid themselves in a big red computer.

20. ROC n ROL

With Tai

By

Wes Fulton

Number 20 of 26 in Series

ROC n ROL

Day-End Stories

By

Wes Fulton

Tai thought she was in heaven.

Tai loved a lot of things about science. She loved doing chemistry in the lab, and looking through a telescope, and digging for fossils.

She was very happy to be chosen by Mr. H to be in his class.

Tai knew that Mr. H liked people in his class to ask questions.

So, Tai wanted to ask Mr. H a very good question.

Tai's question was about her favorite subject, talking with others. She liked to talk with friends no matter where her friends were.

"Mr. H?" Tai asked. "Can I ask you a question?"

"You would make my day with a good question, Tai. Please ask." Said Mr. H smiling.

Tai began her question. "How do different scientists in different countries speaking different languages all talk to each other?" asked Tai.

"I'm impressed, Tai, you made my day." said Mr. H.

"You know how important it is to talk with others about science and not to only work by yourself on something." Mr. H said.

Tai asked "If I could discover a new medicine, how could I tell somebody in another country like Colombia or Vietnam about it?"

"Every medicine has a chemical formula based on math." said Mr. H. "Now let me ask you a question, Tai."

Tai smiled and nodded her head to say yes. She liked questions as much as Mr. H.

"What other names do we use for water?" asked Mr. H.

"Agua." said Tai immediately.

"Yes, agua is the Spanish name for water. Can you think of another name for water?" asked Mr. H.

"H – 2 – Ohhh." Tai said.

Mr. H liked the way that Tai stretched out the letter O when she said her answer. He spun around twice and said "BINGO!"

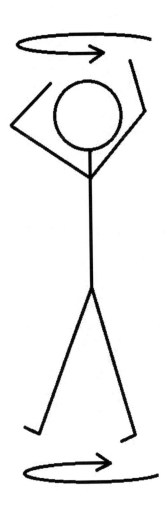

Tai was confused. "Why did you spin around twice and say bingo, Mr. H?" asked Tai.

"That was because I got excited when you said H – 2 – Ohhh, but it has nothing to do with the game of bingo that your grandmother plays." Mr. H answered.

Tai held her belly and laughed and Laughed, because she had never seen Mr. H spin like that, but she also wondered how Mr. H knew that her grandmother did indeed play bingo.

Mr. H continued "When we say H – 2 – Ohhh for water we are talking about water's math formula."

Tai was surprised. "Water has a math formula?" she asked.

Mr. H went up to the board and wrote "H2O" on it with a small number 2 and capital letters for the letter H and the letter O.

$$H_2O$$

"Using the formula for water, H2O, is how a scientist in Vietnam or Colombia or India or China or Brazil or Sweden or the United States or any country knows when you are talking about water." said Mr. H.

He said, "Math is the language of science shared by everyone around the world."

Mr. H went back to the board and drew a picture with 3 circles each with a dot in the middle, one circle for each atom in the smallest thing that could still be called water. What he drew was 2 little atoms of hydrogen connected to 1 bigger oxygen atom in the middle.

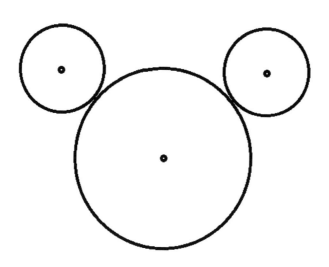

"That looks like a little head with ears." said Tai.

"Indeed, it does look like a little head, but does it think? I think not." said Mr. H and he smiled at Tai again.

"The H2O formula gives a recipe for water. The H2 tells that there are two hydrogen atoms and the O says there is one Oxygen atom." Mr. H said. "Two parts of hydrogen and one part of oxygen makes up water."

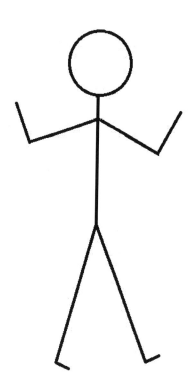

Mr. H continued "Water can change into different forms like a shape-shifter. Regular water flows downstream. Very cold water turns into ice. Very hot water becomes steam. Scientists study the ROC between different forms of water."

"The rate of change from one form of water into a different form of water helps people make the right equipment for a job in water or ice or steam." he said.

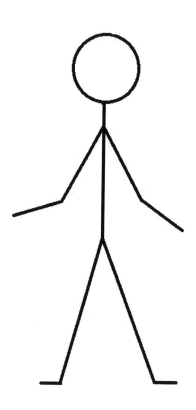

Mr. H wanted to get back to Tai's first question she had at the beginning. He asked Tai "Can we talk about things like atoms to other kinds of life on other planets way out far away from us in outer space?"

Tai was surprised by Mr. H's question. She shrugged her shoulders and just said "I don't know."

"We can, and we did already try to do it with math." said Mr. H.

"Years ago, some very smart people sent a message about atoms of hydrogen into outer space, and it is still going further out. They used the math description for hydrogen. It was part of Voyager."

"What is Voyager?" asked Tai.

Mr. H spun around twice again and said "It is getting late in the school day. We will talk about Voyager some other time."

The ringing of the school bell sounded the end of the school day. All the students left to go home.

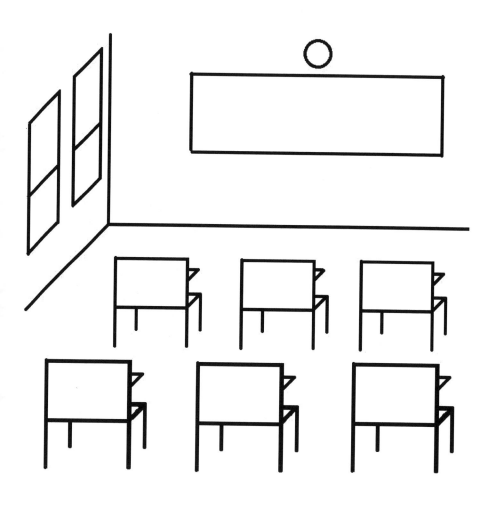

Tai hugged her pillow all that night. She was dreaming about travelling in outer space inside a nice spacious warm rocket ship while petting her pet dog named Voyager.

21. ROC n ROL
With Ulan

By

Wes Fulton

ID Number 21 of 26 in Series

ROC n ROL

Day-End Stories

By

Wes Fulton

Ulan woke up as he was walking in his sleep.

"Wow!" said Ulan to himself. "I was asleep, and when I woke up, I was already on my feet and walking." He started worrying that there might be something very wrong about him.

Ulan's mother woke up when she heard Ulan moving around. Then she came into his room.

"It is almost time to get up to go to school. Are you okay, honey?" asked Ulan's mother. "Did you have a nightmare?"

"Well, I was dreaming that I was walking on top of a partial math formula. It was missing something. I was just about ready to step off into the missing area when I woke up, but I wasn't scared." said Ulan.

Ulan's mother didn't say anything, but she had a surprised look on her face. She helped Ulan get ready for school by bringing his books and his lunch.

At school, Ulan was sitting outside waiting for Mr. H's class to start because he wanted to ask Mr. H something.

At the start of Mr. H's class, Ulan immediately raised his hand.

"Ulan, we are just starting and already you have a question. That is fantastic!" said Mr. H, and then he asked Ulan "What is your question?"

"You have told us a lot about the rate of change, the ROC." said Ulan as he stood up.

"Yes, it is very important in science." Mr. H said.

Ulan continued "You also said that ROC has other names like *durvatuv* and *dafrench*."

Mr. H responded "Yes again. In books on math you will see long words like de-riv-a-tive and like dif-fer-en-tial instead of ROC, but they are all equal. They mean exactly the same thing."

Ulan scratched his nose and said "Yesterday, you mentioned something called partial ROC. What is partial ROC?" asked Ulan.

"It is super good, Ulan, that you remembered something I mentioned very quickly yesterday. Why did you think of it?" asked Mr. H.

"Well," Ulan said and then he looked around the classroom at the other students. "Nevermind." he said and sat down.

Mr. H could tell that Ulan did not want to talk further and said "Okay, Ulan, we will be talking about partial ROC later. It's time for recess."

During recess Mr. H went over to Ulan who was sitting by himself.

"You stopped asking your question a little while ago." said Mr. H to Ulan.

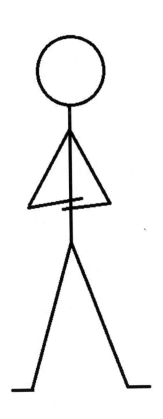

"I didn't want everyone to know what I was going to say." Ulan said.

Mr. H looked into Ulan's eyes and said "People tell me stuff like that all the time, and I never repeat it. Can you tell me?" he asked.

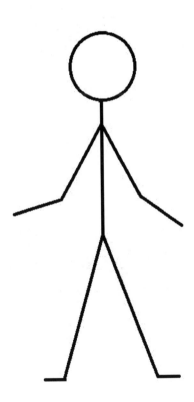

"I woke up this morning and I was already walking." said Ulan.

"Oh yeah, I've done that myself. It surprised you, didn't it?" asked Mr. H.

Ulan smiled. He didn't feel so strange anymore about waking up while he was walking if Mr. H had done the same thing.

"Now do you want to know about partial ROC?" asked Mr. H.

Ulan sat straight up and said "Yes!"

Mr. H started "There could be several different things affecting ROC at the same time. Take weather for example."

"Suppose we are looking at weather. Now the temperature, and the air pressure, and how wet the air is, and the wind, and other things together all have an effect on the weather rate of change." Mr. H said.

Ulan was paying attention, so Mr. H kept talking. "It helps our understanding sometimes to focus on one of those things, and pretend the other things are not changing even though we know they are changing."

Mr. H stopped talking and looked at Ulan. Ulan stared at Mr. H for a few seconds. "That's all?" asked Ulan.

"That's all." said Mr. H. smiling. "That's all it is. Partial ROC sounds harder than it really is."

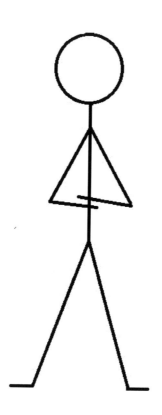

Ulan was really smiling now, and he got up to return to class.

"Ulan, remember." Mr. H said.

Ulan looked at Mr. H wondering what he was going to say.

"Whatever reason you have to think there is something wrong with you, other people have the same thing. You are never the only one, and it is usually just normal." Mr. H finished.

Ulan thanked Mr. H. and went back to class. After Ulan got back home, he read about sleep-walking before going to bed. That made him sleepy.

Ulan slept through the night dreaming that he was a weather reporter on a partially cloudy day. He was right in the middle between a sunny day and a rainy day.

22. ROC n ROL

With Vandita

By

Wes Fulton

Number 22 of 26 in Series

ROC n ROL

Day-End Stories

By

Wes Fulton

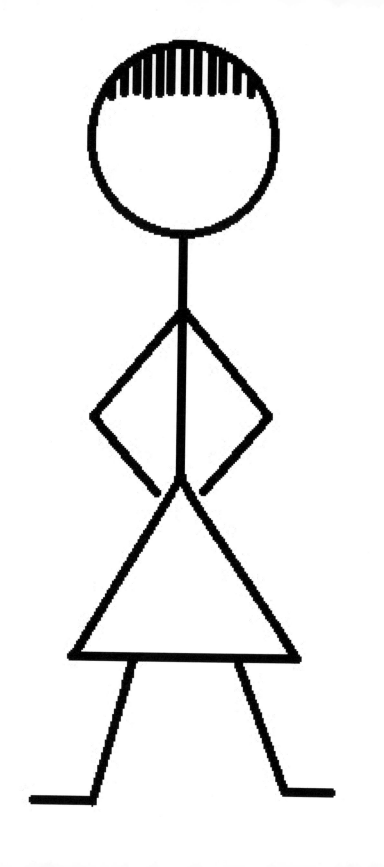

Vandita wanted to control everything.

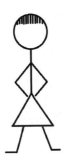

Vandita wanted the temperature to be just right all the time.

If her bedroom temperature was 1 degree too high, then she lowered the thermostat setting for her bedroom so her room would cool down.

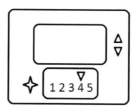

If her bedroom temperature was 1 degree too low, then Vandita raised the thermostat setting for her bedroom so her bedroom would warm up.

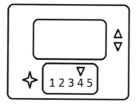

She spent a lot of time messing around with the thermostat setting for her bedroom.

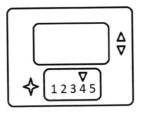

Vandita was forbidden to touch the thermostat in Mr. H's classroom at school.

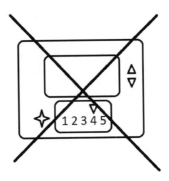

In class she would look at her friend, Grace, with an unhappy face whenever she was a little too cold or a little too hot.

Mr. H told Vandita "You must get comfortable at different temperatures, because we can't change the thermostat every minute. Not only that, but everyone is a little different and wants a different temperature anyway. Try putting on or taking off a sweater or something."

She made a frown with her lips when he told her that. "Okay, Mr. H, but I don't like it when the temperature is too cold or too hot." said Vandita.

Mr. H just smiled at Vandita whenever she made that frown with her lips. That made Vandita even more uncomfortable.

One day Vandita was riding in the back seat of her father's car.

Vandita watched the speedometer in front of her father to follow the car's speed.

She also watched the speed limit signs on the side of the road.

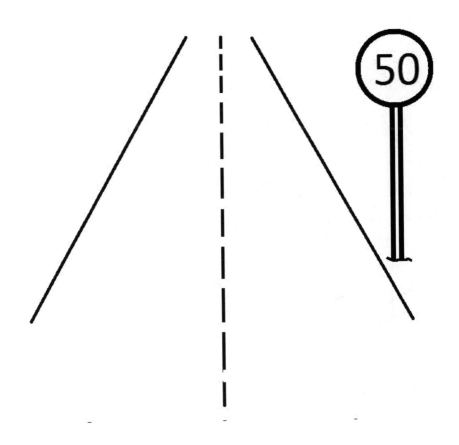

Vandita noticed that her father was going a little too slow. His speed was a little tiny bit lower than the value on the speed limit sign.

"Speed up, Daddy." said Vandita. "You are going too slow!"

Vandita's father decided to teach Vandita a lesson, because he knew how much Vandita liked to control everything.

Vandita's father lightly pushed on the accelerator pedal to go faster.

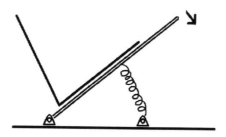

In a short time, Vandita noticed that the speed was a little tiny bit higher than the value on the speed limit sign.

50

"Slow down now, Daddy, you are going too fast! You are above the speed limit." said Vandita.

When Vandita's father went just below the speed limit, she would tell him to go faster. When he was just above the speed limit, she would tell him to go slower.

This speeding up and slowing down kept up for quite some time ... slower ..., ... faster ..., ... slower... , ... faster.

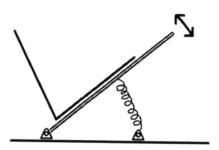

Each time Vandita's father would make the change just a little more quickly than the time before ... slow, fast, slow, fast.

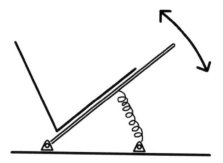

When the car slowed down that pushed Vandita forward in her seat. She had her seat belt buckled, so her body had to slow down when the car slowed down.

When the car speeded up, Vandita was pushed back in her seat.

The slow, fast, slow, fast speed of the car pushed Vandita forward, backward, forward, backward in her seat over and over again each time a little faster.

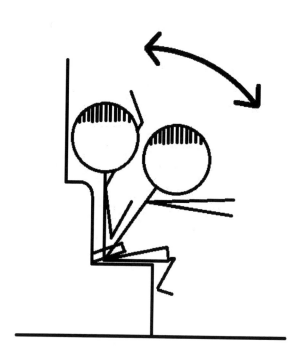

Vandita's head started to feel dizzy.

"Stop the car!" Vandita shouted "I'm getting dizzy."

Vandita's father asked her "Why are you getting dizzy, Vandita?"

Vandita was getting so dizzy that she couldn't think straight and couldn't answer her father.

"How about if we just go at a nice safe speed that isn't changing. Would that be okay with you, Vandita?" her father offered.

"Okay." was all that she could say. She felt a little queasy in her stomach. She settled back in her seat and stopped talking.

The next day at school, Vandita went up to Mr. H at the front of his classroom to ask him about her car trip with her father.

She told him about speeding up and slowing down over and over and quicker and quicker.

"You were in a limit cycle, Vandita." Mr. H said.

"Uh-oh." said Vandita. She didn't know what a limit cycle was, but it sounded bad.

"A limit cycle happens when you try to control things too closely." Mr. H said. "One way to help is with more tolerance."

Vandita liked the sound of more tolerance.

Mr. H added "Other things can help, like sending the ROC value from the output back to the input to give feedback." Vandita thought that feedback sounded like taking a horse's dinner back to the store.

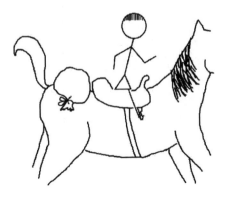

"For feedback, the input value (which is what you want) can be compared to the output value (which is what you get) and also compared to the rate of change, ROC, for smoother control." Mr. H said.

Vandita had heard enough. "Thank you, Mr. H." she said.

She decided to stop messing around with her bedroom temperature and just put on or take off a sweater instead. At night she pulled her bed covers up around her chin and fell asleep quicker than ever before. She had crazy dreams about a horse chasing after her when she was taking his dinner back to the feed store. The horse stopped Vandita and pulled some money out of his saddle to pay for the dinner. Vandita gave the horse back his dinner without taking the money, and the horse gave Vandita a ride back to the stable.

23. ROC n ROL
With Willray

By

Wes Fulton

Number 23 of 26 in Series

ROC n ROL

Day-End Stories

By

Wes Fulton

Willray was a rebel.

Willray would try to do things differently just to be different. So, he rode his bicycle backwards.

When other people were walking slowly, Willray would run fast.

Willray did not watch the TV shows that everyone else watched. He always watched something on TV that was unusual like a mystery or a magic show.

He liked to make other people think by saying something different that they didn't expect him to say.

Willray liked Mr. H's class, because Mr. H encouraged Willray to be himself.

Mr. H would say "Be yourself, because everyone else is already taken."

Mr. H told his students that a writer named Oscar Wilde first said something like that many years ago.

Willray went to school always hoping to learn something new.

Today in class, Willray would find out something completely different.

Mr. H started the class with "Goodbye, everyone."

All the students looked at each other totally puzzled.

"What?" asked Mr. H, and he pretended to be surprised by the puzzled look on all their faces.

"You are starting the class today by saying goodbye." Willray said from his desk near the front of the room.

The students whispered among themselves about the possibility of Mr. H leaving their school.

"Don't leave!" said Ning. She started to cry.

"Ning, oh no ... I'm not leaving." Mr. H said.

Ning stopped crying. Then she asked, "But why did you say goodbye just now?"

Mr. H said, "I just wanted you to think about reversing."

"I'm going to count." said Mr. H., and he counted out loud "1, 2, 3, 4." He looked at the class and then said, "Now who can reverse the last thing I did?"

"4, 3, 2, 1." said Willray.

"That's it, Willray." Mr. H smiled and gave a thumb's up sign to Willray. "It is sometimes called reverse or inverse."

Mr. H continued "we have talked all school year so far about ROC, rate of change, right?" he asked.

The class responded with "Yes." and "Oh yes." and "All year long." and "We didn't talk about much else" and so on.

"Okay, okay." Mr. H said "So we talked a lot about ROC, but it is the basis of higher math and you are finding out about it before many people thought you could. Let's start with an example of ROC and after that we will reverse it."

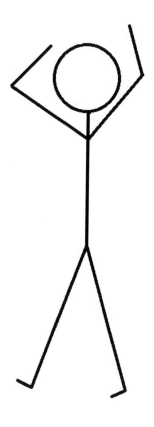

Mr. H asked the class "If I travel 10 city blocks in my car within 2 minutes, then what is my rate of change?"

All the students in the class took 10 and were dividing by 2, but Willray said the answer first. "5 blocks per minute is your ROC." said Willray.

"Quite right you are." said Mr. H. "My ROC is 5 blocks each minute, and I can also call it my speed."

He continued "Now, if I tell you the time at my speed, can you tell me where I am? Can you tell me what my location would be?" Mr. H asked.

Nobody answered for a long time, but finally Willray spoke.

"We don't know how to get location from speed." said Willray.

Mr. H said like reciting a poem ...

"The last thing you did was ROC, speed.

Do reverse of last to get what you need."

"But first let's do the ROC, then we'll reverse." Mr. H said. "Take a person with 10 fingers. If you divide fingers evenly between two hands, that is 5 fingers on each hand." Mr. H went to the board in front of the class. He wrote "10", and on the right side of that he wrote a slash character ("/") to indicate divide, and then after that he wrote "2". He put an equal sign to the right of that, and then he wrote "5" at the end. "Dividing here gives us the ROC answer of 5 that Willray got." he said pointing to the 5.

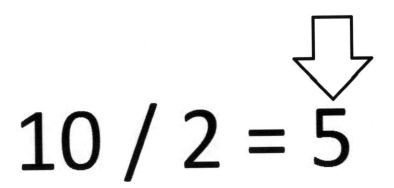

"Now let's reverse." Mr. H left the first equation and started writing on the board just underneath the first equation. He wrote "5" and then multiplied it this time by "2" to get "10" as the answer. He said "Travelling for 2 minutes at speed of 5 blocks each minute, I get 10 blocks as my location. I multiplied this time instead of dividing. Reverse of last, ROL."

$$10 / 2 = 5$$

⇩

$$5 * 2 = 10$$

Mr. H explained "If my speed is 5 blocks each minute, and I go at that speed for 2 minutes I will be 10 blocks from where I started."

Now most of the class could see how to get location from speed.

"Reverse of last we did." said Mr. H.

"Clever we are." Mr. H said.

"Why are you talking like the little green Jedi warrior, Yoda, from the Star Wars movie?" asked Willray.

"Reverse did we." said Mr. H. "Just like Yoda with words it is."

Willray was still pumped up about this reversing thing as he was falling asleep that night. He wanted to know more about ROL and how it combined with ROC. There seemed to be something missing though, but he did not know what it was. He was determined to find out from Mr. H tomorrow. Willray suddenly found himself running through snow on an icy planet with strange machines aiming their lasers at him. He dove for cover in an abandoned rocket ship that must have crashed years earlier. Waiting patiently for help to arrive, he found a secret compartment that opened when he touched the lock. There were rolls of rock candy inside. The rock candy started playing rock and roll. Then Willray knew for sure he was in a dream.

24. ROC n ROL
With Xylia

By

Wes Fulton

ROC n ROL

Day-End Stories

By

Wes Fulton

Xylia liked to pay tolls.

Of course, Xylia was very young. She did not pay tolls with her own money.

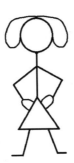

Xylia's mother gave her money from her purse to pay tolls.

What Xylia liked was to hand the money to the toll collector.

Even better she liked to throw the money in the big toll basket at the toll booth.

On the toll road near her house, the toll was only collected going in one direction. Coming back the other direction was free.

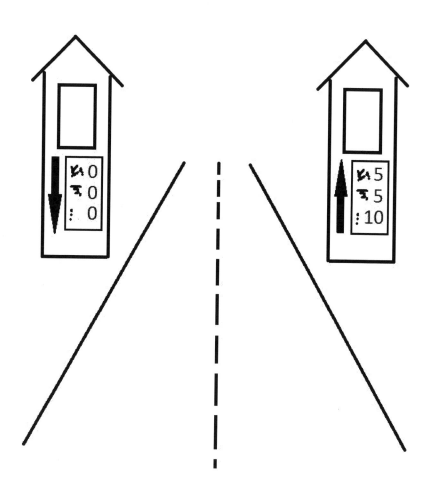

Xylia paid the toll going one way, but coming back, unfortunately for Xylia, there was no toll to pay.

Xylia was one of Mr. H's students in school.

She saw Mr. H in his car on the other side of the same toll road coming toward her and waved to him.

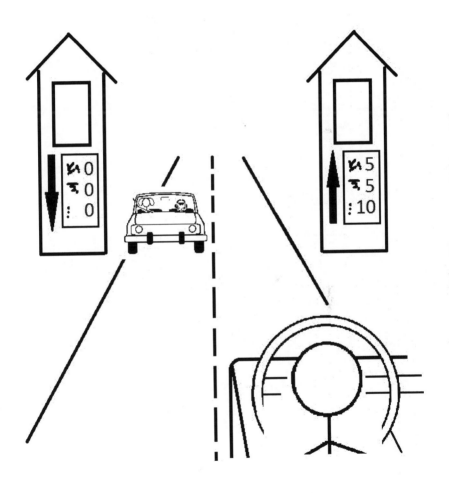

Mr. H waved back and shouted out of his window "See you in school, Xylia."

The next day, Mr. H smiled at Xylia when she came into his classroom. She sat down at her desk near the front. "Did you get to pay the toll, yesterday, Xylia?" he asked, and Xylia nodded yes.

Then Xylia stood up and asked "What are we talking about today?"

"We are still talking about ROL." said Mr. H. He addressed the entire class "What is ROL, class?" he asked.

"Reverse of last." everyone said.

"Yes, reverse of last, or ROL for short, is very useful." said Mr. H. "ROL is the reverse, or more properly the inverse, of ROC."

If we know the ROC, rate of change, then we can find the ROL." Mr. H said. Then he made his face look sad and pretended to be unhappy. "But there's a catch, something I didn't tell you about before." he said.

"What is a catch?" Xylia asked.

Mr. G explained "When you are trying to do something, a catch is something that makes you do a little more. The catch here, going from ROC to ROL, is we need to add a piece of information. We don't need to do that going the other way from ROL to ROC."

"We need to add some extra information that makes reverse of last useful." said Mr. H.

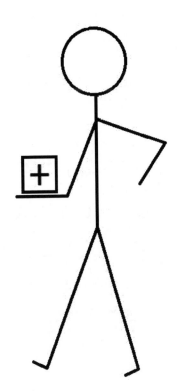

Mr. H looked around the room at all his students. They all looked confused.

"You all look confused." said Mr. H. "How about an example? Would that help?" he asked.

Each student nodded their head in agreement.

Mr. H continued "We already have this example with a car that went 10 city blocks in 2 minutes, right?" he asked.

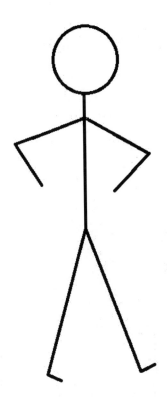

The class responded with "Yes." Mr. H continued, "The ROC, the speed, was 5, and we found that from dividing 10 by 2, right?" The class responded with "Yes, Mr. H."

Then Mr. H said "We didn't need to add anything. We just used amount of change and the time." While Mr. H was talking, Xylia was trying to imagine a car going 5 city blocks every minute. She knew it could not have been during rush hour.

"Now reverse of last, ROL, is going back the other way from speed back to location. We have speed and time and we multiply 5 by 2 to get 10 blocks of location change. We just did that. Are we finished?"

"Yes." said Xylia. "Now we know there was 10 city blocks of change in position from start to finish."

"That is almost right, Xylia." said Mr. H.

Willray was sitting next to Xylia, and all of a sudden Willray stood up. He knew what the missing thing was, the thing that bothered him about the ROL before. "The missing thing, it's the starting point!" He said.

Mr. H was not at all surprised that Willray came up with the correct answer. Willray seemed to look at things a little differently than the other students.

Xylia smiled at Willray. She had always been impressed with his spirit of individual freedom and his independence.

"Thank you, Xylia and Willray." Mr. H said. Then he looked directly at Xylia, and smiled at her again. He asked "Where did I see you yesterday, Xylia?"

"On the toll road." said Xylia with a smile.

"Do we pay on that toll road in both directions?" asked Mr. H even though he already knew the answer.

Xylia answered "No, we only pay in one direction." She knew what was coming.

Mr. H continued "The relationship between ROC and ROL is like that very same toll road. Only going from ROC to ROL do you need to add the starting point. Going from ROL to ROC, a starting point isn't needed."

Xylia looked at the toll road differently on her way home from school. She fell asleep that night dreaming about passing by 100's of toll booth baskets and throwing giant fluffy coins in their direction. The coins all floated down slowly into each basket.

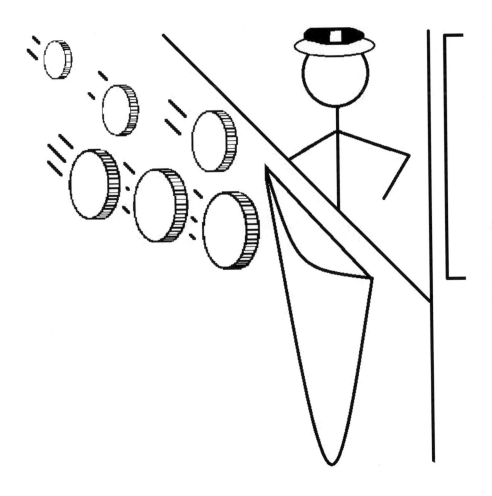

25. ROC n ROL

With Yasin

By

Wes Fulton

Number 25 of 26 in Series

ROC n ROL

Day-End Stories

By

Wes Fulton

Yasin was sad and happy at the same time.

It was the end of the school term, the last day.

That made Yasin happy, because he would be out of school for a while and he wanted to play with his friends more.

Still, Yasin was sad, because he was going to miss Mr. H's class.

Mr. H looked especially very happy as he entered his classroom. He noticed everyone looking at him with surprised looks.

Mr. H laughed "You know why I'm so happy don't you?" he asked and looked at each one of his students.

"It's because you don't have to teach us for a while. Isn't it?" Yasin asked.

"Oh no!" Mr. H said right away. "I like being your math and science teacher."

Mr. H said, "I am going to be a little sad not being in front of you going back and forth with questions and answers for a while."

Now Yasin did not know what to think. Yasin was sad for the same reason that Mr. H just gave for being a little sad.

Yasin asked himself "Mr. H could not possibly be happy for the same reason that I have for being happy, could he?"

Yasin asked "Then are you happy because you will be playing with your friends more?"

Mr. H laughed. "That is partially right, Yasin. You made a very good guess." he said. "Believe it or not, teachers do have a few friends."

Yasin was proud that he made a good guess.

"The main reason that I'm very happy is that I am absolutely thrilled with how much all of you have learned so far. That is why." said Mr. H.

"I mean, just look at how far you have come since we started." Mr. H said.

He went on, "You now know about rate of change, ROC, and reverse of last, ROL." He wrote them on the board.

ROC

ROL

"This is not a small thing." Mr. H continued "Engineers and scientists must know the same thing to do their work."

"The people who built and sent the Voyager spacecraft out into space used ROC and ROL in the design." said Mr. H.

"Those smart people put a message of math on Voyager in case she was discovered by someone from another planet. The message had the math description for hydrogen." Mr. H said.

Mr. H continued "Bridge builders and marine biologists and game programmers must know this ROC and ROL stuff."

"GAME PROGRAMMERS?" exclaimed everyone in the class all at once.

"Okay, so now I have your attention." said Mr. H. "Yes, to make games realistic and fun, the programmers have to use ROC and ROL."

Mr. H explained "The simulation of a car chase in a video game will not look real without modeling the starting and stopping and turning correctly with ROC and ROL."

"But that is not all." Mr. H said "ROC and ROL are involved with just about any kind of thing you can think about. What about money?"

"MONEY?" everyone said at the same time."

"Oh yeah." said Mr. H "Financial markets must account for ROC and ROL as well."

"Car design, medical equipment, construction, manufacturing, and delivery of service all take ROC and ROL into their consideration," said Mr. H "but in most high-level books they use different names."

"Grown-ups like to use long names." Mr. H said. "In most books ROC is called <u>differential calculus</u> and ROL is called <u>integral calculus</u>. They use <u>constant of integration</u> instead of <u>starting point</u>, but none of that is any different than what you have already learned here."

"Now let's get serious." Mr. H said. He went over to his desk and sat on the top of it facing the students.

"For most of this long break from school, you will not be thinking about what we have been studying all of this term." said Mr. H.

Mr. H continued "You will not be thinking about arrays or about partial ROC or about wavy motion or about methods of control."

"What will you be doing?" he asked the class.

Everyone in the class started speaking at the same time. "Baseball!", "Swimming!", "Movies!", "Camping!", "Games!", "Vacation!", "Parties!", "Soccer!", and "Travelling!" were shouted.

"Okay, okay!" Mr. H laughed. "Have fun." he said. "Just remember that ROC and ROL will be with you involved in everything you do."

Mr. H grabbed his books and said, "Take care and be safe." He walked out of the school with his students.

That night Mr. H went to sleep early so he could go fishing early the next morning. He dreamed about being back in class and his students were doing the teaching.

26. ROC n ROL

With Zetta

By

Wes Fulton

ROC n ROL

Day-End Stories

By

Wes Fulton

Zetta didn't say much in Mr. H's class.

Zetta did take to heart all of Mr. H's words, and she did finish every bit of her homework.

She knew about ROC and ROL.

Zetta practiced going from rate of change to reverse of last, and then taking it back the other way.

She had the good fortune to be in a family that loved to travel, and with the hard work of her father and mother they were able to travel.

Zetta met lots of new and interesting people when she travelled. In addition to her native language, she also tried to learn the local languages of the people she saw wherever she went.

Zetta knew a little bit of German, and a little bit of French, and a little bit of Yiddish and Arabic to go along with her very good English.

Zetta could speak Spanish and Italian and Portuguese well because they had a lot of similarity between them.

She was working on learning some Korean, and Japanese, and Chinese, and Hindu.

Zetta was starting to feel at home wherever she travelled.

Her favorite thing was travelling to places she had never seen before.

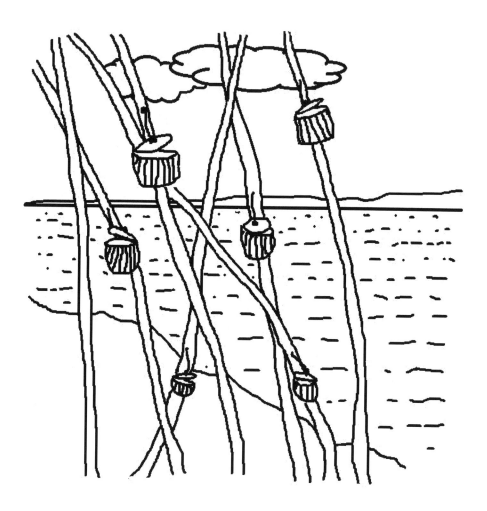

Zetta's brother worked for an aerospace company in a country far away from where she lived. The aerospace company was working on sending mining equipment to asteroids between Mars and Jupiter.

Zetta's family was on a trip to visit her brother.

Zetta's brother was quite a bit older than she was.

He had his own car, and he lived in his own apartment near the aerospace company where he worked.

Zetta wanted some day to have freedom to live and work and take vacations like her older brother.

She decided to try and get all the schooling she possibly could, so later when she was older, she could get a good job like her brother had.

Her brother wanted to take Zetta on a tour of the place where he worked. He picked her up in his car and drove her over to the aerospace company.

There were lots of nice cars in the parking lot of the aerospace company. Zetta and her brother walked from the parking lot to the main company entrance.

Her brother showed Zetta where the raw material came into the company's manufacturing building. There were large sheets of steel, and thick long rods of aluminum, along with large boxes of raw material for making plastic parts.

Zetta saw lots of manufacturing machines on the factory floor arranged in neat rows with space in between them for moving parts and materials back and forth. There were clearly marked walkways for safety.

Her brother took Zetta to the assembly area where small parts are put together with other small parts making bigger parts.

After the tour of the company, Zetta and her brother went to the big break room with lots of tables and chairs where the aerospace company workers relax while eating lunch or taking a break.

The company president came into the break room to meet Zetta.

"Hello, Zetta, it is so nice to meet the sister of my favorite employee." said the company president while he was shaking Zetta's hand.

Zetta answered "Nice to meet you. My brother always speaks highly about you."

"I hear that you have received a very good training so far in this very early part of your schooling." the company president said.

"My teacher, Mr. H, tried his best to do that." said Zetta.

"Very interesting." said the company president. "Tell me about what you learned so far, Zetta." and he took a seat in front of her so he could listen to her carefully.

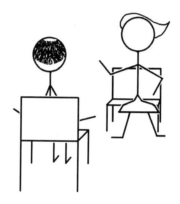

Zetta and the company president talked for over an hour.

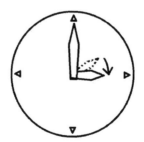

She told him about ROC and ROL and wavy motion and control and partial ROC and limit cycles and equations.

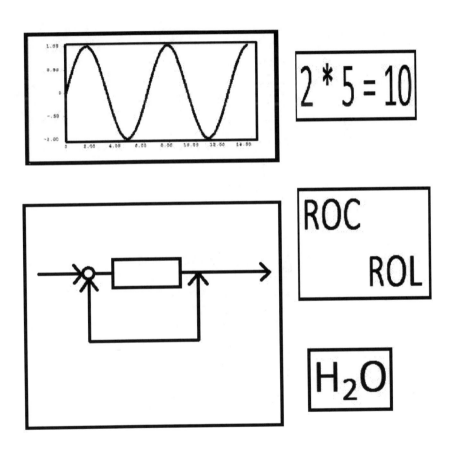

At the end of the conversation, the company president stood up and shook Zetta's hand again.

Zetta's brother went out of the break room with the company president for a few minutes and then her brother came back in to the break room smiling.

"He wants to offer you a job, Zetta!" said her brother. "You already know enough to start working here at the aerospace company."

"But he can't offer you a job because you are so young." her brother said and then he laughed out loud. "You really impressed the company president. He really likes you."

Zetta smiled. She was happy that the company president liked her. She was also glad she was too young to start working. She had so much more to learn from Mr. H, and she liked seeing her friends at school, and she had more travelling to do.

The company president went to sleep that night dreaming about hiring Zetta to work for his aerospace company when she got older. His dreams were not going well. He offered hundreds of diamonds to Zetta, but she just said, "Thank you, but I already have a better offer." He offered her 5 beautiful gold sailboats with sails made of silk. She said, "No thank you, I have too many of those already." He offered her 10 houses on 10 different beaches each with 10 bedrooms and 10 bathrooms. She said, "The 20 private islands I own are already enough for me, no thank you." He offered to give her the aerospace company. She said "Okay."

THE
END

Made in the USA
Columbia, SC
16 July 2021